# Empath

*3 in 1*

## *Energy Healing Guide to Thriving as a Highly Sensitive Person*

# Table of Contents

*Empath Healing: Survival Guide for Empaths, Become a Healer Instead of Absorbing Negative Energies*

*Reiki Healing for Beginners: Improve Health, Increase your Energy and Raise your Vibration*

## *Crystals and Gemstones: Guide to Healing Illnesses with The Power of Stones*

# Introduction

Being an empath can be something that is both truly wonderful and scary all at the same time. All too often the special abilities that an empath possesses can cause as many problems as they can help to solve. One of the main differences between empaths who struggle and those who thrive is a deeper understanding of what it means to be an empath. This book will explore the true nature of being an empath, as well as the different types of empathic abilities that exist. This will help you not only determine if you are an empath, but it will reveal the exact type of empath you are. Furthermore, this book will provide useful information with how to hone and harness your empathic skills, thereby helping you to get the most from your abilities. It will also explore several methods for helping you to stay grounded, thus preventing your empathic nature from taking you too far from the physical plane. By the time you finish reading this book you will not only be able to decide what your abilities are, you will also know how to use them in a way that is fulfilling, enriching and that creates the wonderful life that you deserve.

# Chapter 1:  What Is an Empath?

The term 'empath' is one that has become more commonly recognized in recent years for several different reasons. Most people probably know the term from pop culture sources, such as TV, movies and even literature. There have been numerous fictional characters to receive the moniker 'empath,' although the accuracy of their portrayal is a matter of debate. Another reason why many people are familiar with the term is an increase in the popularity of personality tests. While some of these tests focus on personality traits as defined by psychology, others focus on other traits, such as psychic abilities, spiritual paths and the like.  It is among these personality tests that the empath name is used to define a specific type of person, namely someone who is highly in tune with their intuition. Needless to say, how an empath is defined differs widely from one source to another, leaving the average person asking the simple question, "What is an empath?" This chapter will address some of the common misconceptions of empaths, while also presenting the basic characteristics that actually make up what an empath truly is.

## Popular misconceptions of an empath

Empaths in popular culture cover a whole range of characteristics, abilities and personality traits. Although most of these depictions are positive in nature, many are highly exaggerated, if not completely baseless and unrealistic. This stands to reason since most movies, TV shows and books are more interested in creating exciting, alluring characters rather than exploring the true makeup of a real-life empath. Nevertheless, it is important to understand the difference between the pop-culture empath and the one that actually exists.

The first misconception is that an empath can read minds like you would read a book. This notion gained significant popularity with the character Deanna Troi from Star Trek the Next Generation. In the show, Deanna Troi came from a race of empaths known as Betazoids. Members of this race could not only read minds, but they could communicate with each other telepathically as well. Deanna was only half Betazoid, however, meaning that her powers were only half as strong. Ironically, she was only able to sense strong emotions due to her mixed heritage, which actually makes her more of a true empath than the show's depiction of people who are basically telepathic.

Another misconception in pop-culture is that empaths somehow completely understand their ability and fully know how to use it. All too often an empath will not only sense danger, but they will know that what they are feeling is a warning, not merely a reaction to the environment, something they heard or even something they ate. Even when they are in the midst of a conversation or an event they are actively engaged in they are able to easily distinguish between the emotions of others and their own emotional experience. Furthermore, they always know the exact meaning of the emotional red flag they are receiving, making it seem as if the universe was whispering in their ear. Unfortunately, this isn't how it works.

Some characters take the intuitive capabilities of an empath to a whole new level, going as far as being able to foresee future or faraway events. This can be seen in Star Wars, where Jedi Masters 'use the force' to assess a situation on an intuitive level. Needless to say, being able to sense far off disasters, know when the bad guy is in town or any other similar scenario is a real stretch at best. What is ironic in this instance is that Han Solo more accurately portrays a true empath when he says his iconic line "I have a bad feeling about this." While there is a great deal of debate over just how far a person's empathic abilities can go, the bottom line is that the average empath relies solely on whether a choice or situation feels good or bad.

Finally, there is the fanciful idea that all empaths have mystical personalities, speaking in riddles and hearing the voice of the universe in all living things. Needless to say, this isn't really the way it is. That isn't to suggest that there isn't at least a kernel of truth to this depiction, however, merely that it is so exaggerated as to be virtually unrecognizable from reality. The bottom line is that you may never realize that a person is empathic by their overall personality since many appear as normal as anyone else. Empaths who are more in tune with their emotions may seem more mystical since they are more inwardly focused than the average person. Alternatively, they may seem less mystical and more self-absorbed or even just detached. Thus, the idea that empaths have their own language and recognize each other by their aura is complete fiction and should be recognized as such.

## The true nature of an empath

Just because the pop-culture depiction of empaths is exaggerated and fantastic doesn't mean to suggest that empaths aren't actually something to be admired. The fact of the matter is that a confident, well-functioning empath is someone who stands out from the crowd, not only in terms of personality but also in terms of ability. Although empaths need to use spoken words to communicate and they don't hear the voice of the universe as such, they still possess certain skills, which can make them seem otherworldly at times.

One ability common to empaths is that of being able to get an accurate first impression of a person. This is a skill that just about anyone would pay good money to acquire. While it may not be as flashy as telepathy or predicting the future it can go a long way to avoiding getting taken advantage of by would-be con artists and the like. The biggest problem with first impressions is that most people try to 'impress' you when you meet them. They will be friendlier than normal, more poised than normal and will leave you believing that they are capable and trustworthy overall. Empaths, however, are not so easily fooled. Rather than relying on the physical senses to determine a person's character, empaths use their intuition. This means that they see past the words a person says, sensing what lies beneath.

This leads to another real aspect of empaths — trust issues. These aren't the usual trust issues between one person and another, rather they are the issues faced when an empath's intuition is telling them something completely different from what their rational mind is telling them. First impressions are a great example of this conflict. Again, most people put on their best appearance when meeting someone for the first time, and this can make them seem super friendly, highly reliable and generally very decent. While this can fool the intellect, such a show can never fool intuition. As a result, an empath can get two first impressions of a person, the one they think and the one they feel. The challenge is in believing the intuitive impression. After all, it's very difficult to trust a bad feeling about a person who appears completely safe and good. Subsequently, many empaths struggle with trusting those feelings that defy outward appearances.

Another common skill among empaths is the ability to sense the energy of a situation. At first this may seem like something from pop-culture, however, it actually makes more sense when you examine it closely. The main tool that an empath uses is their intuition. This intuition can sense the emotions of another person, making them as real as the empath's own emotions. That said, any situation contains a particular energy of its own, made up of the energies of all people involved in the situation. It's a bit like noise. A single person speaking will make a certain amount of noise, noise that your ears can easily hear.

Likewise, a crowd of people talking will make similar noise, albeit louder and more chaotic due to how many conversations are going on. Nevertheless, your ears can easily hear that noise too. Energy acts in the very same way. An empath can sense the energy of an individual, as well as the energy of a situation. In this way they can sense when a situation is negative in any way, such as dangerous or potentially sinister.

In the end, an empath is simply someone who has a more heightened intuition, which enables them to perceive things that the physical senses cannot perceive. While this may seem mystical and otherworldly to some, it is commonplace for those with the ability. Although this ability can have many positive applications the sad truth is that it can cause as many problems as it can potentially solve. Thus, as well as being highly gifted, empaths are usually quite conflicted, making their lives extra challenging as well as extra special.

# Chapter 2: Are You an Empath?

The chances are you aren't reading this book because you wanted to better understand what an empath is. Instead, you are probably reading this book because you want to better understand *who you are.* Although the last chapter only touched on some of the basic elements of what an empath is and what an empath isn't you may have resonated with enough to move on to the next question — namely, are you an empath? This chapter will list sixteen different questions that will help you to discover whether or not you are a real-life empath. As you read each question take the time to carefully consider your answer. The more accurate your answers are, the more accurate the conclusion will be. So, without further ado, let's see if you are in fact a bona fide empath! Are you/do you:

## Prone to bouts of anxiety or depression?

Anxiety and depression are key signs of an empath, specifically because they are so in tune with their emotions. While most people are focused on the external world, empaths are usually wholly focused on their internal world. This makes them far more susceptible to extreme moods, both positive and negative. While others can find countless things to distract them from their emotional state, empaths are constantly aware of their emotions. Thus, it's not as though empaths are necessarily more emotional than everyone else, rather it's that they are more aware of their emotional condition at any given time.

Another reason why empaths are prone to bouts of anxiety or depression is the constant flow of emotional traffic they have to deal with. Just as the average person can hear the noise of the people around them an empath can feel the emotions of those around them. Many people tune out noise by putting on headphones or ear buds and listening to music. Unfortunately, empaths can't just tune out emotional input that easily. As a result, they feel all of the stress and anxiety of those around them in addition to their own emotional state. Needless to say, this increase in stressful energy is enough to create real problems.

While depression is a fairly natural condition, experienced by most people from time to time, empaths can tend to suffer from it on a more regular basis. One reason for this, as with stress and anxiety, is that an empath can feel the depression of others. Overexposure to other people's depression can impact an empath's emotional state in a very negative way. The easiest way to tell the difference between normal depression and empathic depression is context. If you feel depressed for no reason, meaning that no event or trauma has caused you to feel that way, then you might be an empath.

## Overwhelmed in crowded places such as the movies or the mall?

Many people love to go to malls and other places in order to experience the energy of large crowds of people who are having fun. In a way they get inspired by such high energy environments. Other people, however, aren't as fond of crowds and their energy. This is especially true of empaths. The number one reason for this is that the more people an empath is around is the more emotional input they are subjected to. Just as the chaos and noise of a crowd can cause a normal person's mind to spin out of control, the emotional energy of a crowd can cause an empath's entire being to spin out of control. Therefore, if you feel overwhelmed in crowded places you might be an empath.

This isn't to say that you have to hate crowded places altogether. There are times when an empath can get their batteries charged from crowded places, although these are very specific circumstances. An event that induces generally positive energy is an example of this. Such events can include concerts or other situations that lack anxiety due to competition, frustration and the like. This is why sporting events can be dangerous since they can generate as much tension and stress as any positive feelings. However, even the most positive crowd is a crowd nonetheless, and many empaths struggle with exposure to crowds of any kind.

## Drawn to healing, helping and care-giving fields?

More often than not the metrics used to determine the empathic nature of a person are negative in nature. However, there are just as many positive metrics that can be used as well. One such metric is whether or not you are drawn to fields of healing, helping and care-giving. Being in tune with other people's emotions makes an empath highly aware of another person's pain and suffering. Subsequently, any job that helps to alleviate pain and suffering would be a natural draw to an empath. Therefore, if you find that you are allured to such professions as the medical field, psychology, relationship counseling and the like you are probably an empath.

This might seem like a bit of a paradox since placing an empath in such an environment would place them under extreme emotional stress. Unfortunately, this is one of the dangers inherent with empaths seeking such jobs. By getting emotionally attached to the people they help, empaths can become emotionally drained very quickly on a regular basis. Even so, the process of improving a person's health and wellbeing seems to compensate for this, since a person's emotional state improves with their physical and psychological state. This is why empaths can function well in such environments. Therefore, if you are the type of person who feels better when other people feel better, you just might be an empath!

## Sensitive to the emotions of others during childhood?

Childhood is challenging enough for just about everyone. Empaths, as you might by now expect, have an even tougher time. This is because in addition to having to deal with the emotional volatility of being a child, empaths have the added burden of sensing the emotions of the people around them. One way that this manifests is in the area of guilt. As a child you no doubt did numerous things that upset your parents. The average child would feel somewhat guilty for such wrongdoings, however, an empath will feel enormous guilt. This is because you can sense the pain or anger of your parents. If every falling out with your parents was an emotional tidal wave for you it probably means you had the tough task of growing up as an empath.

Another sign that a child is an empath is the number of people who confide in them. The simple truth is that by feeling other people's emotions an empath can understand exactly what that person is going through. Such an understanding makes them seem years wiser than they should be. As a result, people of all ages are drawn to them, sharing their deep secrets as well as regrets, hopes, fears and every other important thought or feeling that they might have. If you experienced such incidents of others opening their souls to you it means you were recognized for your empathic abilities even at a young age.

**Prefer time in nature, alone or with animals over being with people?**

This question is related to the one regarding crowds. The thing with crowds is that a person can hate them without being an empath. However, if you prefer time alone, in nature or with animals instead of being with other people, then you are probably an empath. This is especially true if you hate being in crowds too!

Empaths love nothing more than a long, peaceful walk in nature. Understandably, the main reason for this is the lack of human interaction. Although it is widely known that even trees and plants give off energy, the fact is that this energy is of a different nature to that of human emotions. The energy in nature is calming, refreshing and rejuvenating in essence, meaning that it restores a person rather than wearing them down. As a result, empaths are usually drawn to nature, even choosing to live in more rural areas in order to surround themselves with nature's restorative energies.

Animals, like nature, lack the emotional complexity and chaos of people. Subsequently, empaths will usually choose to spend more time with animals than they will with other people. At first glance this may seem antisocial in nature, however, it simply comes down to a matter of self preservation. While empaths enjoy time alone they can become depressed when isolated for too long. Animals can be the perfect solution by providing non-human company that takes the loneliness out of solitude. As a result, many empaths have cats or dogs in their lives that they lavish with love and affection.

Finally, there is the aspect of alone time. Some people cannot stand being alone for long periods, finding the solitude and quiet as disturbing as empaths find noise and crowds. In contrast, an empath will not only desire alone time, they will actually need it in order to stay balanced. If an empath is deprived of time alone their stress levels will begin to rise dramatically, reaching dangerous levels if the situation persists. Empaths can become emotionally volatile as a result, lashing out in fits of anger and rage at even the slightest of things. Alternatively, they can express their emotional fatigue through bouts of crying that come on unexpectedly and for no apparent reason. All that is needed to set things right again is a decent dose of solitude. If this sounds like you, you are almost definitely an empath.

**Struggle with establishing boundaries or saying "No" to others?**

A common phenomenon found within anyone who possesses an inherent skill or talent is that they also possess the corresponding desire to put that talent to use. This is particularly evident in the case of empaths. More often than not, empaths will not only attract those with difficulties who need someone to confide in, they will also actively seek out such people. Unfortunately, this can lead to a problem that manifests within most empaths, namely the inability to say "no."

If you struggle with establishing boundaries, or simply saying "no" to those in need you aren't gullible or spineless, rather you are probably an empath. The fact is that by feeling the pain of others you take on the need to comfort and resolve that pain. Therefore, no matter how tired you are you will always commit to helping someone in need. Furthermore, you will probably give of yourself on a level that most people would draw the line on. This takes the form of lending people money, even when you barely have enough for yourself, letting someone move into your home or any other form of help that serves to affect your life in a very real way. If any of these situations seems familiar it probably indicates that you are a true empath.

## Tend to feel drained by the people in your life?

Most people like to spend time with others in order to restore their energies. This can take the form of large and loud parties, or it can come in the form of smaller, more intimate gatherings. Either way, most people come away from social interactions feeling more energized than when they went in. In the case of an empath, however, the opposite is usually true. Rather than feeling energized by others, empaths will tend to feel drained by the people in their lives.

One of the main reasons for this is that people either send energy out or they take energy in. You can think of this as either being a radio transmitter or a radio receiver. Those who are receivers soak up the energy of those around them, becoming stronger and more vibrant as a result. In contrast, those who send energy out become drained by those around them, especially when most of them are receivers rather than transmitters. Empaths are a strange breed, possessing both the ability to transmit as well as the ability to receive. Thus, they can come away from a social gathering having absorbed all of the negative energy while also having transmitted all of their positive energy to everyone else. As a result, empaths will usually feel drained by the people in their life.

## Experience random mood swings?

Random mood swings are a common symptom of any empath, causing them to seem quirky at best and emotionally unstable at worst. The main reason these mood swings cause concern amongst non-empaths is that they occur for no apparent reason. Most people judge life by what their physical senses perceive, therefore things are always as they appear. Empaths, in contrast, experience life on an emotional level, meaning that they perceive the unseen energies that underlie physical reality. As a result, empaths can become overwhelmed by negative energies that the average person can't sense, let alone see. This can cause an empath to have instant and unexplained mood swings anytime, anywhere.

The most common of these mood swings is sadness or depression. When an empath is in the presence of stress, anxiety and sorrow their demeanor will take on those traits. Even though they aren't unhappy themselves, an empath can't help but absorb the energy around them. Thus, their mood will change depending on their environment. If this happens to you, don't be alarmed, rather than being unstable you are actually demonstrating a trait of being an empath.

## Feel the emotions of others, as though the experience is yours?

A common misconception about empaths is that they are simply regular people who feel a deeper sense of sympathy for those who are suffering. This understanding, or rather misunderstanding, is what causes so much frustration amongst those who want to help empaths when they are feeling overwhelmed. What the average person fails to understand is that there is a huge difference between sympathy and empathy. Feeling sympathy is when you feel bad for someone else who is suffering. Empathy, on the other hand, is when you actually feel the emotions of others, as though those emotions were your own.

This means that you actually share the experience on an emotional level, even though you don't on the physical level. Which is why, as an empath, you have a hard time walking away from those in need.

Although this trait usually manifests itself in a negative way, causing an empath to share the pain, sorrow and suffering of others, it can also manifest itself in a more positive way. Empaths can also share in the joy and excitement that others feel. Such circumstances, although rarer in nature, can go a long way to restoring an empath's energies. As a result, many empaths have learned to seek out environments where the emotional charge is positive in order to balance and restore their own emotional wellbeing.

## Have a general need for solitude?

More often than not an empath will find themselves in an environment that is defined by such negative emotions as fear, sorrow, anger and stress. This is due to the fact that these emotions are much stronger than contentment or peace, therefore they overwhelm any environment the same way a bad smell can overwhelm the air of a large room. As a result, empaths have a general need for solitude. By spending time alone an empath can not only avoid negative energies from the outside, but they can also take the time to discover the true condition of their own emotional state. This allows them to recognize any issues they have to address in their lives in order to restore balance and wellbeing to their hearts and minds.

Another reason why empaths need solitude is just to stop the flow of emotional energy from the outside. Needless to say, the constant flow of negative energy that bombards an empath can leave them feeling depressed and drained. However, positive energy can also have that effect after a while. In a way it's a bit like noise. Even the most pleasant of noises can become irritating after a while, causing a person to seek out silence in order to rest their ears. Likewise, solitude serves the purpose of soothing an empath's mind from any and all energy. If you are drawn to solitude there is a good chance it's because you are an empath.

**Experience anxiety from noise, smells and excessive talkers?**

Although empaths experience life on an emotional level, this doesn't mean that they don't use their physical senses just like everyone else. On the contrary, not only are empaths acutely aware of their physical senses, but the input received from these senses can impact an empath more than the average person. While sensory input usually goes straight to the intellectual mind of the average person, the same input goes straight to the emotional mind of the empath. This means that instead of analyzing this input an empath feels it. The word most commonly used to describe this state is sensitivity. As a result, most empaths are far more sensitive to such things as noise, smells and excessive talking.

If you find that you become easily stressed and anxious from strong odors, loud noise or the constant chatter of non-stop talking this suggests that you are probably an empath. This can actually cause nausea in the case of smells, seeing as you are more sensitive to such input. However, the most common physiological effects are headache, panic attacks and general irritability. This is because your heart rate is increased, as is your adrenaline production. After a while these factors will begin to cause your body and mind to become agitated, so much so that you will be unable to focus or think clearly until you are able to find a place of solitude where you can recover your emotional equilibrium.

## Adversely affected by bright lights?

In addition to smells, sounds and excessive talking, bright lights can also cause a great deal of distress to an empath. Again, this is due to an empath's increased sensitivity to sensory input. When exposed to bright lights for a short time an empath can feel a bit disoriented, agitated or just anxious due to an increase in adrenaline. However, if the exposure is prolonged, or the light is extremely bright, an empath may experience symptoms as extreme as migraines, heart palpitations or even nausea. Unfortunately, the correlation between such symptoms and bright light is not something that most people would think of, resulting in empaths being misdiagnosed or simply undiagnosed altogether.

When you understand how such conditions affect an empath the symptoms become much easier to recognize and address. If you ever feel this way in brightly lit environments you need to take action as soon as possible. Needless to say, the first choice would be to remove yourself from the environment altogether. However, if this isn't possible you should do what you can to reduce the effects of bright light. A good option is to carry a pair of softly tinted sunglasses that will reduce the light without making indoor environments too dark. Simply knowing why you have the symptoms is only half the battle. Taking care of yourself when those symptoms occur is the other, and perhaps most important half.

## Have a hard time going to sleep before midnight?

Sometimes empaths can demonstrate symptoms that are shared with other personality types. Insomnia, for example, is one such symptom. Most people link insomnia with an overactive mind, especially the type associated with such personalities as problem solvers, inventors and even worriers. While these personalities do experience insomnia on a fairly regular basis they aren't the only ones. Empaths can have a hard time going to sleep, usually as a result of the emotional overload they experience during the day. Such an overload increases stress and anxiety, which in turn makes it harder to fall asleep and drift off into peaceful, contented slumber.

One of the easiest ways to tell the difference between empath insomnia and the other forms is the amount of activity going on in the conscious mind. Inventors and problem solvers will struggle with sleep since their brains are mulling over details about plans, projects or the like, thus keeping their minds too active for sleep. Even worriers will be playing their greatest fears over and over again in their minds, thus keeping them from peaceful sleep. However, an empath can have trouble falling asleep even though their conscious mind is relatively calm and at peace. This suggests an emotional cause rather than an intellectual one. If this sounds like you it means you are probably an empath.

## Feel the presence of otherworldly spirits?

This might be a topic you have trouble sharing with the people in your life, especially those who aren't empaths. After all, how many people in your life would react well to you telling them that you can feel the presence of otherworldly spirits?! Unfortunately, as already discussed, most people experience life through their physical senses alone, meaning that their experience is limited to those things that can be seen, heard, touched, smelled and tasted. While there have been numerous reports of spirits creating smells, temperature changes and the like, the chances are the average person wouldn't be sensitive enough to recognize such signs, let alone realize what they actually meant.

Fortunately (or unfortunately, depending on your point of view), empaths are capable of perceiving otherworldly spirits through non-physical means. Since spirits are made up of energy, it stands to reason that empaths can sense them the same way they sense other people's emotions. The biggest problem is in not knowing what such sensations are all about, which can create significant distress and anxiety in an empath who senses a spirit without understanding the event. That said, if you have ever felt 'not alone,' don't panic. You aren't having a mental breakdown, instead you are probably sensing another being that simply lacks physical form.

## Love trees, mountains or the ocean?

As you might expect, empaths are often drawn to places where people are in scarce supply. These places include forests, mountains and large bodies of water such as oceans. The obvious reason for being drawn to these places is that it provides an empath with some much needed solitude. By spending time away from people empaths can recharge their emotional batteries, giving them the strength to cope with the emotional overload they will face when they return to society.

There is, however, another reason why empaths love these natural sanctuaries, one that the average person simply wouldn't understand. Places such as mountains and oceans seem to defy humanity, proving the power of nature over the power of man. Oddly enough, empaths tend to find comfort in this truth, feeling a sense of relief that the overwhelming world of man does, in fact, have its limits, limits which cannot be overcome. As a result, forests, mountains and oceans are something of a sacred space for empaths, a space free from human incursion and development.

## Go above and beyond in all your relationships?

When it comes to relationships, the tendency for empaths to go above and beyond reaches all new levels. This stands to reason when you consider the fact that empaths are willing to do whatever it takes to rescue perfect strangers from their pain and suffering. How much further will an empath be willing to go in order to rescue a loved one from similar pain and suffering? The answer is quite a lot. Because empaths care even more for the emotional wellbeing of loved ones they will do anything they can to help maintain their relationship with them, even when that effort isn't reciprocated. This is because they know the pain that letting the relationship fail will cause, and if there is one thing an empath cannot do it is willingly cause pain to another person.

Another reason why empaths are so willing to over-invest in relationships, both of a romantic nature as well as platonic relationships, is that they are far more forgiving of any wrongs done to them. Because an empath relates to the emotions of others they also relate to the fallibility of others. Thus, when a

something that would drive
away, an empath will identify
and thus forgive their partner the
want to be forgiven if the roles were
unfortunately, this often results in
remaining in unhealthy relationships for far
ng, causing them even greater pain and
ering in the long run. If this has happened to
you, then you just might be an empath.

## What your answers mean

If you are an empath, the chances are you identified
with most, if not all of the questions presented in
this chapter. This is because these questions are
based on the actions of an empath due to their highly
intuitive and emotional nature. However, this
doesn't mean that you have to answer 'yes' to all of
the questions in order to be a real life empath.
Certain questions may apply to one type of empath
over another, so answering 'no' to some of the
questions doesn't take away from the chances of you
being an empath. In short, if you identify with at
least half of the scenarios described you are
doubtlessly an empath. The next question to answer
is exactly what type of empath are you?

# Chapter 3: General Types of Empaths

Being an empath is a bit like being an artist. While art is fundamentally about self-expression there are many forms that it takes, such as painting, sculpture, dance and the like. The same can be said for empaths. Although the fundamental reality of being an empath remains fairly the same, there are several different types of empath that a person can be. The questions in the last chapter can help to narrow down which type of empath you are, however it can be easier to make that determination by comparing each of the types against your own experience. This chapter will discuss six different types of empath, showing which qualities are unique to each. With this information you will be able to identify the exact form of empathy that you possess, and how it can apply to your day-to-day life.

## Emotional Empath

Emotional empaths are the most common type of empath, and the most basic. This is the variation that most people identify with when they think of the term 'empath.' As an emotional empath you will be able to sense the emotions of those around you, thereby knowing what a person is feeling regardless of their outward appearance. The ease with which you can sense the emotions of others can be both a blessing and a curse. Although it can be a good thing to know what another person is truly feeling, the truth is that you can sense the emotions of others as easily as you sense your own feelings. This can make it difficult to differentiate between the two at times, causing a fair amount of emotional confusion as a result.

To say that you can sense other people's emotions may actually be understating your experience somewhat. The fact is that you cannot only sense how others are feeling, but you can share in those feelings as well. Again, this can cause significant confusion with regard to your actual emotional state. You will probably experience mood swings as a result of how others are feeling, and this can make you seem unstable in extreme cases. Subsequently, it is important to develop the ability to differentiate between the emotions of others and your own feelings. This will help you to stay true to your emotional state regardless of the environment you are in. Additionally, by remaining detached you can prove more beneficial when helping those around you since you aren't allowing your own energies to be altered or drained by their emotional experience.

## Physical/Medical Empath

The second type of empath is the physical/medical empath. If you possess this type of empathy you will be able to sense another person's physical health and wellbeing. Essentially, the experience is the same as with an emotional empath, however, instead of being able to tap into another person's emotional state you are able to tap into their physiological state. One way this takes shape is that you get an image or a sense of something that is wrong. For example, if someone has a chronic illness, such as diabetes, the word 'diabetes' might appear in your mind, seemingly out of nowhere. Alternatively, you might actually be able to feel the symptoms of another person the same way an emotional empath can feel another person's emotions. This can be very distressing if you don't know what is going on since you may experience numerous symptoms throughout any given day, even though you are in perfect health yourself.

Some physical/medical empaths can actually see issues in another person's energy, such as blockages, imbalances and the like. This is where practices such as Reiki can prove a very beneficial profession, as such an empath could use their abilities to detect and help correct a person's energy issues. For the most part, people in this category choose medical professions where they can use their intuition to help diagnose and cure the patients they see. Needless to say, the same detachment that can benefit emotional empaths can go a long way to benefiting physical/medical empaths as well. After all, you can't be of much use to others if you think the symptoms you feel are yours rather than theirs!

**Geomantic Empath**

Geomantic empaths are those who can sense the energy of a place, landscape or environment. If you have ever experienced a strong emotional response to being in a place you might be a geomantic empath. However, this is only true in the case that the environment is relatively free of people. After all, if there are many people in an area you might actually be picking up on their energies, which is what an emotional empath would do. Geomantic empaths, in contrast, feel the energy of an environment that is relatively deserted, meaning they are feeling the energy of the place, not of other people.

One example of this can be found in nature. As a geomantic empath you will feel a deeper sadness anytime you witness trees being cut down or patches of natural land being developed for human use. The sorrow you feel for such an event would be similar to the sorrow an average person would feel for a tragedy in which numerous lives were lost. Essentially, as a geomantic empath you identify all life as equally sacred and the fact that you feel the energy of natural environments only strengthens that fact.

There is another form of experience for geomantic empaths, one that involves 'energy fingerprints.' Anytime you feel extremely sad, frightened, happy or angry when you are in a place it could point to the energy imprint left by countless people who had specific experiences in that place. For example, an old jail might make you feel depressed and sad, whereas an old theater might make you feel happy and excited. This is the result of the emotional fingerprint left by those who were there when the place was active. All in all, if you are a geomantic empath it is important that you leave places that make you feel uncomfortable and spend time in places that bring you peace and joy, such as forests, beaches and other natural environments.

## Plant Empath

One of the things that most empaths discover at some point in their lives is that the energy that flows through humans is very much the same as the energy that flows through all of nature. Therefore, it will be no surprise to discover that there is an actual form of empathy that specifically focuses on plants. If this form describes you then you are a plant empath. Like a physical/medical empath you are able to sense and identify the physical wellbeing of those around you. However, in this case instead of people it's all about the plants around you. This means you have an intuitive green thumb!

As a plant empath you can feel the actual needs of the plants you come into contact with. To the outsider this can seem as though you are keenly observant, capable of discerning a plant's health by even the most subtle of signs. However, the truth is that you only find those signs because you know what to look for. This can make you very capable working in such places as parks, nurseries, or for any type of landscaping company. Not only will you be able to detect problems early on, but you will also know intuitively how to address those problems, using techniques that most others wouldn't even have thought of.

If you are a plant empath you probably have numerous plants in and around your home. This is because healthy plants give off energy that is rejuvenating to an empath, regardless of type. By nurturing plants to their optimum health you are actually helping to create an environment that benefits you as much as you benefit the plants.

Although some might scoff when you talk to your plants or hug your trees you know that such actions are as natural as when two people talk to each other or engage in an embrace.

## Animal Empath

Most empaths feel a closer bond to nature, resulting in them having more plants and animals in their lives. However, an animal empath takes this bond to a whole new level. Much like a plant empath, animal empaths are able to sense the condition and needs of any animal they come into contact with. One of the main differences between plants and animals, however, is the depth of communication that can occur between animals and animal empaths. While plants can communicate needs and conditions, animals can communicate feelings, thoughts and even desires. Make no mistake, just because an animal can't express their thoughts with the spoken word doesn't mean that those thoughts don't exist.

If you are an animal empath you will have an almost telepathic ability with any animal you meet. Not only will you be able to sense their feelings and thoughts, you will also be able to transmit your feelings and thoughts to them. As a result, animal empaths make the best veterinarians, pet sitters and animal psychologists. Most actively seek out jobs in such areas since helping animals is a very real part of an animal empath's design. Furthermore, like physical/medical empaths, animal empaths can detect illnesses in an animal, making it possible to treat animals more quickly and effectively as a result. The only downside is that most animal empaths will become fairly antisocial, choosing to spend their lives with animals over people due to the connection they have with the animal kingdom.

## Claircognizant/Intuitive Empath

Finally, there is the type of empath known as the claircognizant/intuitive empath. These empaths are capable of not only sensing the emotions of other people, but of actually perceiving other people on an intuitive level. This means they can receive information from another person just by being around them. Scientific studies have demonstrated the possibility of this phenomenon, specifically as it relates to the actual nature of thoughts. It turns out that thoughts are comprised of energy, making it possible for them to be perceived much the same way that emotions are. The single difference is that claircognizant/intuitive empaths seem to pick up on energies of a more conscious nature, such as thoughts, intentions and personality traits.

The main advantage that claircognizant/intuitive empaths have is that they can perceive a person's true identity quickly and easily. This means that they know what a person is like regardless of outward appearance or even their emotional state. Subsequently, they are able to get the most accurate first impressions of a person. In more extreme cases claircognizant/intuitive empaths can all but read another person's mind, making them virtually telepathic. Unfortunately, this level of perception can easily lead to sensory overload. It is recommended, therefore, that claircognizant/intuitive empaths develop the ability to 'turn off' their abilities at will in order to allow them the ability to recharge their batteries. Additionally, it is advised that they carefully choose the company they keep, ensuring that they spend time with people they can trust and feel comfortable around.

## The Takeaway

The chances are one or more of the empath types listed in this chapter resonate with you. Few people possess traits from only one type, meaning that most empaths are a mix of two or more empathic types. You might be an intuitive empath with claircognizant or geomantic tendencies. In the end, the better you understand your abilities, the easier it will be to nurture and use those abilities. Hopefully, this chapter has helped you to not only understand your abilities and experiences better, but to understand yourself in a more meaningful way. Always remember, being an empath is something you should enjoy and be proud of!

# Chapter 4: What Areas Does It Affect Our Lives?

Being an empath is something that affects every area of your life. It's not like a job where you clock in, do your work, clock out and go home. The experience of being an empath is one that takes place 24 hours a day, 7 days a week. Subsequently, there is no area of your life that is left unaffected by your empathic abilities. Although you can't prevent your empathic nature from influencing your life you can manage those influences, thereby taking control from the effects of your emotional environment. This chapter will discuss six different areas that are directly affected by empathic abilities, revealing some of the challenges faced as well as ways to overcome them.

## Health

One of the most common areas affected by empathic abilities is a person's health. The negative effects of the constant bombardment of emotions can be overwhelming at best and devastating at worst. Although these effects cannot be avoided altogether when a person is aware of them they can make decisions and choices that better protect their wellbeing.

Some of the lesser physical symptoms that empaths frequently suffer from include headaches, fatigue and minor panic attacks. These are usually brought on by long exposure to large crowds, noisy environments or any other situation involving harsh sensory input. Such symptoms fade quickly once the empath finds a quiet place in which to rebalance their energies. In the event that they cannot get away, these symptoms can turn into more extreme forms, including migraine, dizziness, nausea and even muscle pain.

In addition to affecting physical health and wellbeing, empathic abilities can significantly affect a person's emotional health and wellbeing as well. Lesser symptoms include a general feeling of sadness, low energy levels and even mild stress and anxiety. Such symptoms are usually the result of being in a negative environment or around people with negatively charged emotions. They can also be the result of becoming emotionally spent due to helping those in need. If left unchecked, these symptoms can turn into more serious issues, including depression, extreme anxiety and even rage in some cases. Needless to say, it is critical that you find a place of solitude in the event that you start experiencing any of these symptoms, as only then can you begin to undo the harmful effects of your environment. Daily meditation will also help to increase your stamina in highly charged emotional environments.

## Addictions

Many empaths find the constant flow of emotional energy that bombards their senses hard to cope with from time to time. While most find healthy ways to deal with these situations others turn to less healthy methods. In fact, some develop addictions in their quest to dull their senses and bring a sense of tranquility to their minds. While some addictions are less harmful than others, the bottom line is that no addiction is truly healthy. Therefore, it is important that you be on the lookout for addictive behavior in your life in order to avoid any long-term, harmful consequences.

One such addiction is eating. This makes a lot of sense when you consider the effects food can have on both the body and the mind. Most eating addictions involve treats or comfort food, things that make a person happy just thinking about them. Thus, not only do foods such as ice cream and cake provide a quick boost of sugary energy, they also create a sense of comfort and peace that helps to restore the mind. From time to time such an indulgence can be healthy, however, when that indulgence turns into addiction it can have very negative effects on both body and mind.

Other addictions include drinking alcohol and smoking. These addictions also make sense seeing as they provide a chemical depressant that helps to dull an empath's senses, thereby relieving them from the inner chaos and turmoil that their mind experiences most of the time. Shopping is another common addiction, one that is less understood than the others. However, it makes perfect sense when you take the time to truly consider it. When a person shops they have the hope and expectation of finding something that will bring joy and fulfillment to their lives. Since empaths often suffer from sadness and even depression, such an expectation will go a long way to raising their spirits. In the end, these addictions are usually nothing more than an empath's way of self-medicating through their more serious bouts of depression and anxiety.

If you experience such addictive behavior it is critical to talk to someone who might be able to help you overcome it. Alternatively, turning to such things as meditation and exercise in place of addictive behavior can actually help replace unhealthy habits with healthier, more beneficial ones.

## Relationships, Love, and Sex

Unfortunately, the empathic nature of a person often results in them finding themselves in the midst of toxic relationships that they simply cannot escape. This dynamic has two main reasons. First, empaths are usually drawn to people who need help, seeing as they have an inherent need to offer support and assistance whenever possible. While this seems like a good thing, the fact is that it can result in empaths being attracted to those who are abusive and even self-destructive in nature. The more damaged a person, the more attractive they are to an empath. The second reason is that an empath cannot abandon someone in need. Therefore, even when they realize their relationship is toxic they become stuck as they can't bring themselves to cause suffering to the other person by ending the relationship. Talking to someone, be it a friend or a counselor, can go a long way to resolving this dilemma.

Another way that empaths struggle with relationships is that they are often emotionally spent, meaning that they don't always have the energy needed to nurture a healthy and loving relationship. This doesn't mean that empaths don't crave deep and meaningful relationships, rather they don't usually reserve enough emotional energy to invest in their own happiness, spending it all on the happiness of others instead. The only real solution to this is for an empath to find someone who is both very energetic as well as very understanding with regard to the empath's plight.

Love and sex are also highly impacted by a person's empathic abilities. While many people see sex as an act that expresses love between two people, empaths often see it as a way to deaden their senses, restoring them to a state of being physically grounded. This can cause tension in any relationship where the other person feels more lusted after than loved when it comes to intimacy. The truth of the matter is that empaths will never engage in an intimate encounter with anyone who they don't love deeply, therefore any intimate activity will always be done out of love regardless of outward appearances. The important thing for any empath is to make sure they demonstrate their love for their partner on a regular basis through any means possible.

**Parenting**

Parenting is a challenging enough experience on its own, let alone when it involves an empath at one end or the other. Even so, every empath alive has grown up as a child with empathic abilities, and countless empaths start families of their own, thus entering the world of being a parent with empathic abilities. The increase of emotional awareness between parents and children can be both a blessing and a curse. It is therefore critical that you become aware of the dangers so that you can better manage the effects of your empathic abilities within your family relationships.

As a parent you will struggle with the flow of emotional input you receive from your children. This is made worse by the fact that children are usually full of conflicting and confusing emotions due to the biochemical changes their bodies are constantly going through. Needless to say, this only serves to increase the chaotic nature of the emotional input, creating a never ending whirlwind in your mind. It is essential that you develop the ability to detach from emotional input in order to protect yourself from becoming completely unhinged as a result of such heightened emotional stimuli. Practicing yoga or meditation on a daily basis can help make all the difference.

One of the positives of being an empathic parent is that you can sense when your children are suffering. This gives you an advantage of being able to make yourself available to them even when they are trying to hide their inner turmoil. Taken too far, however, this ability can turn into a form of privacy invasion, therefore only ever use it as a tool, never as a weapon. If your children refuse the help you offer you need to respect their privacy and let them deal with their situation on their own.

As a child you will find life somewhat more difficult because of your empathic abilities. Every child does things that they regret, things that often cause their parents a certain amount of pain and distress. However, most children are able to put those events behind them rather quickly, moving on to better times. Unfortunately, your empathic abilities will amplify the guilt and sorrow you feel for everything that causes your parents any sort of pain. Even the slightest of things such as a little white lie can cause you to feel absolutely guilt ridden since in addition to feeling your remorse you can also feel the pain your parents experience when you lie to them. This is highly unfair, of course, but it often results in empaths developing the highest of standards in terms of morals and virtue. Developing emotional detachment, however, is highly recommended in order to lessen the effects.

**Work**

Another environment that can impact an empath in a really big way is the workplace. This is particularly true for any job that creates a highly competitive atmosphere. In addition to experiencing their own stress and anxiety, empaths will also experience the stress and anxiety of those around them. This can result in an empath being ten times more stressed out than anyone else at any given time. Needless to say, this needs to be avoided at all costs.

The first rule for an empath is to create boundaries within the workplace. While the knee-jerk reaction is to offer help and solace to those in need, this can prove disastrous if no limits are established. As an empath you need to ensure that you get plenty of alone time to balance your energies and recharge your batteries. The heightened emotional atmosphere within the workplace will drain you faster than any other environment, therefore you need to take extra precautions to ensure your own health and wellbeing.

Perhaps the best case scenario is for an empath to find a job that allows them to be fairly autonomous. Although too much solitude can have its downside as well it can be a better challenge to face than that of being constantly mentally overwhelmed and emotionally exhausted. The important thing is to put your needs first at all times so as to prevent from becoming completely burned out and unable to perform your job adequately.

## Extraordinary Perceptual Abilities

So far this chapter has focused on some of the more negative ways in which empathic abilities can affect your life. Fortunately, there are numerous positive ways in which your life can be significantly enhanced and enriched as a result of your inherent gift. As an empath you may find you have certain abilities that seem almost otherworldly at first. Rather than doubting or even fearing these abilities you should embrace them and develop them so that you gain every benefit that they have to offer.

One thing many empaths experience from time to time is the ability to see future or far off events. Commonly referred to as premonitions, these visions can happen quite unexpectedly, especially when the event doesn't impact the empath themselves. If you have ever seen a place or a person clearly in your mind, only to see that person or place on the news shortly afterward, you have had a premonition. This won't happen all of the time, and not all empaths have this ability. However, if you experience it you should embrace it for the miracle that it is. There probably won't be anything you can do to affect the situation, so don't feel as though you are somehow obligated to save the world. Instead, this is just a situation where your subconscious taps into the collective subconscious and discovers something interesting. The sooner you trust this ability is, the stronger it will become.

Enhanced dream states are another common phenomenon experienced by empaths. This stands to reason as dreams are born of the subconscious, just as emotions and intuition. Therefore, the stronger your skills of intuition and emotional sensing the more intense your dreams will be. At the very least you will have an increased ability to recall your dreams, something the average person usually lacks. However, the chances are your dreams will also be richer in detail, more colorful and even longer lasting as well. Even better, you may experience what are called lucid dreams in which you become aware of the fact that you are dreaming. This opens up a whole new dimension that allows you to experience anything in the dream world with the same intensity as though it were occurring in the real world.

Finally, there are those empaths who have the ability to sense beyond human or personal experience. If you have ever 'read' the mind of an animal, or sensed the needs of a plant you are one of these people. The simple truth is that thoughts and emotions are pure energy by nature, therefore empaths can perceive them regardless of their origin. After all, a thought is a thought, regardless of whether it comes from a person or a tree. Therefore, it should be just as possible to read the one as it is the other. Many empaths don't possess this skill, however, that doesn't mean that their abilities are weaker or less developed. Rather, it's a matter of frequency. While some empaths are wholly tuned in to the human frequency, others are more in tune with the frequencies of nature. If you feel more at home with nature, and you can sense the needs of plants and animals, then this is how your empathic abilities affect your life.

In the end, each person's empathic abilities will affect their lives in different and unique ways. This is because each person's abilities are different, as are the lives they lead. Therefore, what is true for one person isn't necessarily true for another. As a result the most important thing you can do is to discover what is true for you and the methods that work best for you in terms of honing and harnessing your skills. The more in control of your skills you are the more in control of your life you will become. After all, being an empath doesn't have to be confusing and challenging, instead it can be something truly wonderful and fulfilling.

# Chapter 5: Thriving as an Empath — Protect your Energy

Most empaths are driven to give of themselves in order to help restore the happiness and wellbeing of those around them. Unfortunately, this can lead to an empath becoming emotionally, physically and spiritually drained as a result. Even worse, empaths don't always have someone in their close inner circle that they can turn to for help in restoring their emotional energies. Subsequently, it falls on the empath to take the time and effort to protect and maintain their personal energy levels. This chapter will address some of the negative practices that you should give up, as well as some positive practices that you should start in order to take better care of your overall health and wellbeing. Additionally, it will provide some methods that will help you to stay emotionally grounded at all times. By following these recommendations you will not only be able to avoid becoming run down and emotionally drained, you will actually be able to start thriving as an empath.

## Bad Practices to Give Up

As an empath the chances are you have developed a number of habits that serve to undermine your happiness and wellbeing. These habits aren't necessarily bad behaviors, rather they are good behaviors that have no boundaries. This is because empaths usually lack the ability to say "no," meaning that good, noble traits such as being giving and selfless can become all-consuming. Subsequently, it is important to recognize and eliminate these practices in order to maintain your emotional balance, health and overall wellbeing. Bad practices to give up include:

- **Always trying to please others.** Needless to say, trying to please others isn't a bad thing unto itself, however, when left unchecked it can create a situation where an empath over-commits themselves. By always saying "yes" to others you allow yourself to be used continuously, never giving yourself the time and space to restore your energy levels. The result is that you become drained and spent, much like a cell phone that isn't charged regularly. One of the most difficult yet important lessons to learn for any empath is to put their needs first from time to time. After all, you can only help others when you are strong enough to do so. Therefore, by looking after yourself you are ensuring that you can be of service to others.

- **Being an enabler.** Another bad practice that needs to be eliminated from your behavior is that of being an enabler. Unlike trying to please others, however, this behavior truly is bad in nature. The reason why it's easy to enable others to behave badly is that, as an empath, you can relate to why they need to behave badly. Unfortunately, not only does this not help the other person, it also serves to harm you as well. After all, most of the bad behaviors you enable involve how the other person treats you, meaning that by enabling them you only allow more harm to come your way. Therefore, it is essential that you recognize bad behavior when you see it, and rather than enabling it you take a stand and protect yourself from it. You can forgive and accept someone without actually encouraging their negative side.
- **Carrying other people's burdens.** This is a behavior that affects almost every empath at some point in time. Whenever you see someone else suffering, as an empath you feel the need to alleviate that suffering. In the event that you can't actually find a solution to what is creating the suffering you take on the burdens of others in order to make their lives better. While this seems like a good idea at

first it actually is quite the opposite. First, it results in you taking on more burdens than you can handle. In the end, each person should only ever have to carry their personal burdens and no more. The second reason this is a bad behavior is because it enables the other person to continue going in the wrong direction as they don't have to carry the burden of their consequences. Ultimately, you have to let others experience the pains and burdens in their life in order to learn their lessons accordingly.

- **Always taking the blame.** One of the strongest traits of an empath is the unwillingness to cause harm to others. Unfortunately, this trait can result in an empath always taking the blame for when things go wrong, even when they aren't at fault. This can create several problems, both for the empath and for the other person involved. By always taking the blame you allow the other person to avoid accountability for their actions, thus enabling them to behave badly over and over again. Doing so robs them of learning valuable life lessons. Additionally, by always taking the blame you carry the burden of responsibility for other people's actions and wellbeing. The weight of such responsibility will eventually prove too heavy, leaving you crushed under its weight.

- **Feeling obligated to spend time with others.** Another behavior that appears positive but is actually harmful is feeling obligated to spend time with others. This can significantly rob you of valuable alone time in which you recharge your emotional batteries, thereby leaving you vulnerable to emotional fatigue and even depression. Furthermore, you may wind up spending time with people who are highly negative, resulting in your energies being drained and damaged by their negative energy. In order to protect yourself you need to avoid such obligatory behavior, making choices that benefit you instead.

- **Being addicted to victimization.** Sometimes when an empath allows themselves to be victimized over and over again they begin to become defined by the process. After a while they identify with always being drained, depressed and taken advantage of. This can become so ingrained that when an empath begins to feel strong and happy they feel guilty, almost as though they aren't fulfilling their purpose. It is important to remember that your purpose is never to be victimized. Therefore, such things as happiness and wellbeing should be normal for you, not the exception to the rule.

- **Giving energy to those who take it for granted.** This is one of the main ways in which an empath allows themselves to be victimized in the first place. By giving your time, effort and emotional energy to those who take it for granted you will only ever drain your resources with nothing to show for it at the other end. It's a bit like trying to fill a bucket with a huge hole in it. No matter how much water you put in, the bucket will always demand more. Eventually you need to learn to let go of those who take you for granted so that you can give your energy to those who will appreciate it, and thus be more effective as a result.

- **Being codependent.** This goes hand in hand with the previous point. When you remain in a relationship where the other person takes and never gives you will spend all your energy and never get anything in return. Needless to say, this will leave you in a constant state of feeling drained and even depressed. It is critical for an empath to only maintain relationships that are mutually beneficial. Only then will the time you spend with others restore your energies. Any relationship that is one sided needs to be ended for your happiness and peace of mind.

## Good Practices to Start

Discovering and ending bad practices is only half the formula when it comes to creating a life in which you can thrive as an empath. The other half of the formula is to discover and practice those behaviors that benefit you. Again, as an empath you have an increased responsibility to protect and maintain your energies, therefore it is absolutely essential that you perform those practices that will enable you to do so. The following list includes some of the more effective practices that will help you to stay strong and happy under any circumstances.

- **Accept your empathic ability.** As already mentioned in this book, being an empath is not as simple as it is often portrayed. One of the most difficult challenges any empath faces is accepting their empathic abilities. Not only can these abilities be confusing, they can also be distressing if you don't know what they are. However, once you realize the nature of your abilities it is vital that you accept them so that you can align your mindset with them. Learn to hear your inner voice and to trust what it tells you. Only then can you rid yourself of the inner conflict that so many empaths face.

- **Own your gift.** Accepting your empathic ability is only the first step toward creating a rich and fulfilling life. The second step is to own your gift. This is where you take the time to nurture your abilities so that they serve to improve your life. One thing many empaths fail to recognize is that their empathic abilities are for their benefit as well. You shouldn't feel as though you are only meant to improve the lives of those around you. Instead, you should constantly use your abilities for your benefit as well. Learn to discern those you can trust from those you can't, and protect yourself accordingly. Furthermore, use your intuition to know which paths will lead to failure and which paths will lead to the success you so richly deserve.

- **Develop emotional detachment.** Due to the sensitive nature of being an empath, it is vital that you learn to develop emotional detachment. This is the mindset where you can recognize the emotions of those around you without being affected by them. Buddhism and other similar traditions promote emotional detachment as a method of avoiding suffering. By engaging in such practices as meditation and mindfulness techniques you can develop the ability to detach yourself from even the most negative emotional environment, thus protecting you from the harm such negativity would cause.

- **Meditate on a regular basis.** Meditation is probably the most proven technique with regards to developing emotional detachment. Therefore, you should take the time to find a form of meditation that best suits you. Not all forms are the same, therefore if you don't take to one simply let it go and try another. The important thing is that you find one that works for you. Not only will the right meditation help you to become detached, it will also help you to balance your energies, thereby releasing any stress that has built up due to exposure to negative people or circumstances.

- **Practice shouting, running and other forms of catharsis.** Another way to release stress and anxiety due to being exposed to negative energies is to expend it physically. Any high energy activity will help to burn off excess energy, including stress and anxiety. Running or engaging in any intense exercise is a great way to achieve this goal. A less physical alternative is to release energy through such methods as shouting or screaming. These practices allow you to express your emotional intensity, thereby restoring balance and inner harmony. In the end, any form of catharsis that allows you to expel excess or chaotic energy will help to keep you centered and balanced.

- **Develop somatic mindfulness.** Sometimes an empath can lose touch with their personal emotions due to the constant flow of emotions from the outside world. This results in them not attending to their own needs. One way to overcome this is to develop somatic mindfulness. This is a technique where you focus on different parts of your body to determine your emotional state. A tense jaw, for example, is indicative of stress and anxiety. An elevated heart rate can point to anxiety or even anger. Shallow breathing, stiff shoulders and clenched fists can also point to anger, stress and other negative emotions. By taking the time to assess your body you can determine your true emotional state, and thus take steps to correct any imbalances you are experiencing.

## How to Stay Grounded as an Empath at All Times

Staying grounded is something that most empaths have a hard time doing. One reason for this is that they don't take the time to look for or recognize the signs that indicate when they are ungrounded or unbalanced. Even worse, most don't even know what such signs look like. Another reason is that they don't know how to restore balance and stay grounded even when they do recognize the warning signs. This section will discuss how to recognize and read those signs, as well as some proven methods for staying grounded and restoring emotional balance and wellbeing. Signs of being ungrounded include:

- **You have difficulty concentrating and staying focused.** This is a sign of emotional and mental fatigue in general, affecting both empaths and non-empaths alike. As an empath, however, you will probably experience this sign on a more regular basis as your emotional state will tend to become chaotic more often than in the case of an average person. Subsequently, any time you experience this condition it is important that you take the time to step back and evaluate your emotional state. Rather than trying to push through you need to take action to restore your emotional balance and wellbeing.

- **You find yourself being generally clumsy.** In addition to affecting your mind, being ungrounded can also affect your body in a very real way. This can take the form of being overly clumsy, even to the point of bumping into things such as furniture, doorways and even walls. Essentially, this is the same chaotic state for the body as confusion is for the mind. Thus, it points to the condition of being ungrounded. If you experience such bouts of clumsiness it is important to recognize the warning signs and take steps to restoring your peace of mind.

- **You struggle to remember details.** Memory is another mental skill that is directly impacted when you are ungrounded. This doesn't necessarily mean that you can't remember such things as your name or the day of the week you are in, rather it means you can't remember more detailed information, such as appointment times, people's names and the like. Needless to say, many people struggle with details to one degree or another. However, if you struggle to remember certain things even after several reminders it may point to a state of emotional imbalance.

- **Reality and fantasy become hard to distinguish.** The more extreme the state of being ungrounded is, the more extreme the symptoms will become. One example of this is the inability to differentiate between fantasy and reality. In the event that you expect unrealistic responses to your words or actions, or you fail to grasp the particulars of your day-to-day life you need to take a serious time out and restore your mental and emotional wellbeing. This break from reality is the result of being too fixated on your inner world. Left unchecked, the consequences can be quite dire.
- **You find it difficult to complete tasks on time.** Few people can claim to be punctual all of the time, however, when an empath becomes ungrounded this behavior can become quite extreme. In a way, this is related to becoming detached from reality. The inability to recognize and follow time is another sign that you are too focused on your inner reality, thus causing you to be less in touch with the reality of the outside world. If left unchecked, this behavior can also become

quite dangerous, causing all sorts of negative consequences in every area of your life.

- **Other people have a hard time understanding you.** If you have ever spent large periods of time alone you know that your first conversation with another person will usually be labored and even confused. This is because you have become so internalized that your external forms of communication have become wholly unnecessary. If this happens when you aren't alone it probably suggests that you are becoming ungrounded and that you need to take the time to reorient yourself with the outside world around you.

The following are seven effective ways for grounding yourself:

1. **Drumming.** Drumming is a highly effective way of restoring your connection to the outside world. One reason for this is that it actually serves as a calming and restorative influence. The rhythm of a drum resembles a heartbeat, which creates a natural vibration that brings order to emotional and mental chaos. Furthermore, it can create the comforting sense that a mother's heartbeat

has on her unborn child. Another reason why drumming can restore grounding is that it can provide a cathartic release of stress and anxiety, thus restoring balance to your heart and mind. Therefore, drumming can be highly effective whether you choose to simply listen to the rhythm or be a more active participant.

2. **Use essential oils.** Essential oils can help to ground you by shifting your focus to your physical senses. The sense of smell has been proven to be far stronger than previously believed, even challenging sight as the strongest of the five senses. Therefore, essential oils can bring you from your inner world back to the outer world in a fast yet gentle way. Furthermore, certain scents such as sandalwood, cedarwood, patchouli and peppermint have a calming and soothing effect, thus relieving the stress and anxiety that causes you to become ungrounded in the first place.

3. **Keep crystals on your person.** Crystals can help to restore your sense of being grounded by balancing your energies. Unlike drumming and essential oil methods, this method addresses the issue at the energy level itself. Crystals such as garnet, onyx, tiger's eye, hematite and copper have been shown to

be effective in attracting positive energy, blocking negative energy or simply restoring the balance of energy. You can choose to keep such crystals on your person simply by carrying them in your pocket or purse or you can incorporate them into jewelry, thereby adding a sense of artistic flair to your practice.

4. **Restore health and wellbeing to your root chakra.** This is another method that addresses any imbalance at the energy level itself. Taken from the Hindu tradition of chakras, or energy wheels, this method helps restore health and wellbeing to your root chakra which connects you to the Earth. You can restore energy by holding a hand over the area of your root chakra, right at the base of the spine, or you can surround yourself with the color red which will also help to increase vital energy to this area. The stronger this chakra is, the more grounded you will become.

5. **Practice tree exercises.** Most people only think of trees as being beautiful things that reach into the sky. The truth is that trees also reach deep into the Earth, spreading roots deep and wide in order to be strong and stable. Tree exercises, such as hugging a tree, will help you to become grounded once again

by helping you to connect to the Earth through the tree itself. Another exercise is to visualize yourself as a tree, with roots extending from your person to deep underground. This will help you to restore balance to your state of mind by bringing you from your inner self back to the world that is around you and under your feet.

6. **Consume energy rich foods.** Medical science has discovered a strong link between the energy of a person and the chemicals their brain produces. From their point of view, it is those chemicals that determine the nature of a person's energy. There are those, however, who would argue that the truth is the other way around and that a person's energy actually impacts how the brain works. Either way, the notion of the brain affecting energy opens up other options for restoring emotional balance and wellbeing. Certain foods, such as root vegetables, nuts, dark chocolate and protein rich foods can help create chemical reactions that improve how a person thinks and feels. By eating these foods you can begin to feel grounded again almost instantly, especially in the case of dark chocolate.

7. **Find an exercise that matches your energy.** In the end, the main reason why an empath becomes ungrounded is an imbalance in their energy. This imbalance can be caused by a lack of energy, or alternatively, by an excess of energy. In either case certain exercises can help to restore balance by raising energy levels or by burning off excess, anxious energy. Running and martial arts can help to release any pent-up energy that causes a sense of being ungrounded. Gentler exercises, such as riding a bike or practicing yoga, can help to increase or simply realign energies, thereby restoring a person's overall health and wellbeing. The important thing is to pick the right exercise for the right time. For example, riding a bike, while beneficial, won't necessarily burn off excess or anxious energy the same way that running or martial arts would.

While each of these methods serves to restore emotional balance when you begin to feel ungrounded they can also serve to prevent issues from arising in the first place. The best way to ensure this is to implement some or all of these practices into your daily routine. Once you discover the practices that help you the best you should engage in them even when you are feeling strong and well. This will enable you to stay grounded at all times, thus helping you to develop a lifestyle that allows you to thrive as an empath, which is nothing less than what you deserve!

# Conclusion

Now that you have read this book you will have a deeper understanding as to the nature of being an empath. Having empathic abilities can be very challenging, however, with a greater understanding of your skills you will be able to control their impact on your life more effectively. Furthermore, by implementing the methods discussed in this book for becoming more grounded you will be able to avoid the pitfalls that many empaths encounter as a result of letting their abilities go unchecked. The simple truth is that being an empath is a wonderful thing, however, it requires extra effort, awareness and skill. Hopefully this book has provided you with the tools you need to get the most from your empathic abilities. The very best of luck to you as you begin living the life of a truly empowered empath!

# Sources

https://consciouslifenews.com/7-effective-ways-to-keep-yourself-grounded/1183716/

https://www.thoughtco.com/traits-of-empaths-1724671

https://www.amandalinettemeder.com/blog/2014/7/31/13-signs-you-are-an-empath-and-what-it-means

https://www.mindfulnessmuse.com/mindfulness-exercises/increase-somatic-awareness-with-a-body-scan-mindfulness-exercise

http://www.soulandspiritmagazine.com/signs-you-are-ungrounded/

https://theknowing1.wordpress.com/2011/07/01/at-a-glance-30-traits-of-an-empath/

https://www.psi-zone.net/signs.html

https://www.aconsciousrethink.com/2746/17-survival-tips-for-empaths-and-highly-sensitive-people/

https://www.learning-mind.com/types-of-empaths/

https://www.dictionary.com/e/pop-culture/empath/

# Introduction

Reiki healing has been around for thousands of years, though it has only recently piqued a worldwide interest. It is a practice that can be done by anyone with the proper training—and this book is going to provide that for you.

As you read, you will learn about the many benefits of Reiki and how it can heal you physically, emotionally and mentally. You will learn about the theory and the practice, as well as how to heal both yourself and others. As you advance, your ability to heal will become more pronounced and you can even learn to give Reiki to others across a distance.

Finally, this book will touch on some of the other techniques that may be used in addition with Reiki. This will heighten your spiritual connection to the world around you and help you connect to the healing energies of the world. Happy reading!

# Chapter 1: An Introduction to Reiki

Reiki (ray-kee) healing has Japanese origins. The meaning of Reiki is 'Universal Life Force,' being made up of the terms 'rei' (which translates to universal) and 'ki' (which translates to life force). The goal of Reiki healing is generally to access the life force. Once it is flowing freely, it is directed in a way that heals the body.

The energy flow spoken of in Reiki healing comes from a universal force, which is believed to exist in all life forms. If you consider the difference between someone who is dead and living, the simplest way to explain it is that one contains energy, while the other does not. Our bodies are constantly at work, maintaining our breathing and other bodily functions, healing our injuries and sickness and keeping us alive—even when we are sleeping. It is energy that allows this to happen.

## Reiki Healing to Restore the Balance of Internal Energy

Many forms of Eastern medicine believe that illness comes from blocked energy channels. Reiki is intended to remove these blockages and help healing energy flow freely through the body. These blockages often result from a lifetime of experiences—negative emotion like anger, jealousy, fear, greed, and temptation can upset this balance. In addition to negative experiences, our channels may be blocked from not taking care of our physical bodies. Eating a diet that is low in nutritional value, not getting enough water, and being sedentary can also cause blockages in energy. Sometimes, our own minds can also get in the way of the positive energy field, as our doubts about ourselves and the doubts that others have of us cloud our judgment and our flow of healthy energy.

A good way to look at this restoration of energy is to imagine yourself as a hollowed-out pipe that has been left at the bottom of a riverbed. When you come into the world as an infant, you have not yet been harmed by the negative emotions and experiences in the world. Nobody has made you question your self-worth and there is no reason not to believe the world is a good place. As clean water continues to flow through this hollow pipe, things go well. The body is capable of great healing and maintaining a high state of health. Over time, however, the negative energies, thoughts, and general dirt of the world collect inside this pipe. As it sticks to the walls of the pipe, there is less energy flow. Over time, the flow of energy may stop altogether.

## What Can I Expect from a Reiki Healing Session?

Many newbies to the world of Reiki energy and natural healing may choose to work with a professional for their first few sessions. It is important to remember that Reiki sessions only restore the natural flow of wholesome energy through your body. You may be aware of the sensations of energy as they fill you, but you typically notice the benefits after the session. You will notice the benefits in the way that you interact with the negativities of the world around you. You will also notice how the healing energy helps heal you from ailments and complaints, but this happens over time. Reiki stimulates the body's natural healing process. Though many people have Reiki experiences that they refer to as 'miracles,' the reality is that the body and the energy flowing through it cause the healing—not the session itself. Often, it takes time for the effects to begin.

## The Science of Reiki

The research on Reiki is fairly new, though this should not come as a surprise since Western medicine has only started to scratch the surface of more holistic, alternative treatments. While some studies have disputed the presence of this energy, it is believed that Reiki works because of the overall relaxation and healing environment that it provides to the body. By allowing the body to exist in a more relaxed, stress-free state, it encourages the body's natural healing processes. This can be seen in the many stories of miracles of Reiki and how it has healed people—whether their pain was physical, emotional, or mental. Reiki promotes all-over body wellness, unlike Western medicine, which relies on the treatment of symptoms rather than trying to heal the body and encourage long-term health and healing.

## A Brief History of Reiki

The man credited for establishing the Reiki practice of modern medicine is Mikao Usui, a Sensei and Japanese monk. He was the first to publish literature on the topic and establish a basic framework for Reiki practice. Even though this was the first time that Reiki had been regulated, research shows that at least four types of Reiki had been practiced across Japan prior to Usui's work. With this framework came the passing down of knowledge through different generations of monks, healers, and scientists. It is common practice that for someone to practice Reiki, they must receive training from a teacher in the subject. Reiki teachers typically practice themselves and they pass down their knowledge and techniques to students.

According to stories, Usui searched for many years to find a way to heal himself and others through his hands, without having to tap into and deplete his own energy stores. He studied in China, studied Buddhism, and even took a 21-day course on a mountain that involved fasting, meditation and prayer. Usui's quest ended at the end of that 21-day course when he found Sanskrit symbols in the caves. It was not long before Usui would take this knowledge and set up a clinic, helping bring Reiki to the people around him, both teaching others and healing the world. These initial teachings focused heavily on how people could heal themselves, with the belief that people could not use their life energy to heal others unless they first healed themselves. It is recorded that Usui taught 16 different Reiki healers before his death and these healers would carry on his knowledge and teach a new generation of healers.

Modern-day Reiki in the United States was brought by Japanese-American Hawayo Takata in 1937. Born in Hawaii, she spent an extended time in Japan completing Reiki training. When she returned to the United States, she would pass down her knowledge and techniques. Today, its use is widespread across different continents of the world, usually being labeled as a form of holistic or alternative medicine.

# Chapter 2: Benefits of Reiki

One of the biggest questions you may have is, "Why Reiki?" There are dozens, possibly even hundreds, of forms of meditation, yoga and other holistic healing practices designed to promote this overall feeling of wellness and stave off sickness and negative emotions. Even though there are many options, Reiki sets itself apart because of how easy it is—you can do it anywhere, without any equipment, at any time of the day. Aside from the convenience factor, this chapter will go over some of the benefits of regular Reiki practice.

## Increased Ability to Deal with Negative Energies and Stresses of the World

We cannot always control who we interact with. Even in the best careers, we might have to work with people that give off generally bad energies or who take advantage of others. You may pick up negativity from encountering an angry person at the bus stop or the coffee shop. You might even have your own negative emotions to deal with, as feeling saddened or angry at times is part of the human experience.

The benefit of Reiki is that it helps relieve of the weight of any negative experiences you may have. As you walk through your office building or down the street, you will notice a new recognition for those things that do not serve your purpose. You will understand what things do not serve your purpose in life and which encounters leave you in an undesirable mental state. Then, you can learn to block the energies from things you do not want to experience and avoid those situations that you can, should they not promote the satisfied, energized feeling that you should feel.

**Ability to Heal Others**

If you decide to progress past the point of Reiki healing for yourself, it is easy to become attuned with the world and direct your energy in a way that corrects the energy flow of others. As you choose people to practice with, it is important to choose those that are opened to the idea of Reiki healing. You may find yourself put off of the practice altogether if you try it on a relative with health problems who does not have an open mind to new age topics like Reiki. Keep in mind that it is not always your failure. Reiki will not work on someone who cannot open their mind and body to the flow of energy.

## Physical Healing

Physical healing is one of the benefits of Reiki that people seem to be most skeptical about. They do not understand how something that restores energy can help relieve the symptoms of their physical condition, whether it is a simple headache or a chronic illness. Those who doubt this method have often been healed using a Western form of medicine, which commonly focuses on treating the ailment directly instead of using a full-body approach. This is one of the reasons that people turn to alternative or holistic medicine when a more scientific approach has healed them. In many cases, the results have been a complete turnaround. There are even anecdotes of people who have turned to Reiki healing and other alternative medicines and had success in healing cancer, relieving chronic pain, and fighting off severe illness.

## Mental and Emotional Healing

People's pain and sickness are not always visible. Many people struggle with anxiety, depression, repressed emotions, and other mental and emotional states. They may not even be aware of their emotional state or what is causing it. Reiki does not always help you heal emotions unless you deal with them, however, it can make you more aware of your emotional state. This awareness can help you understand your problems. It can also help you tap into the divine nature and understand your purpose in life. As you continue to connect to the energy that exists within everything and all around you, it can help cultivate more positive emotions in your life, including connectedness, love, intimacy, kindness, compassion, and sharing.

## Increased Spirituality

The flow of energy that you experience with Reiki can help you notice the interconnectedness between all the life forms of earth. As you connect to all that is living around you, you will feel a greater connection to the divine. You will also feel as if you are part of something greater than what exists in your immediate world. For many people, this creates the feeling of being connected to something great and powerful. It offers reassurance that you are present in the Universe and you know that you are loved by and connected to the spiritual beings, both living and non-living that you may encounter through your day.

## Greater Compassion

The connectedness that you feel when regularly cleansing and connecting to your internal source of energy can help you find greater compassion for all that exists in the world. You will be more compassionate and empathetic when you encounter others who are in pain, whether emotional or physical. You will also be more tolerant and understanding of others, aware that you cannot possibly understand their specific situation. As you learn this deep compassion for others, you will also learn to be kinder to and have greater compassion for yourself. This can help heal people who struggle with emotional trauma or low self-esteem, as they often struggle with treating themselves as well as they would treat others.

## Stress Relief

Stress relief is a major benefit of Reiki, as it is responsible for many of its effects. When you regularly relax and provide yourself with stress relief, it gives your body and mind a much-needed break from the fast-paced world around you. This stress relief can help you sleep better at night and promotes a stronger immune system since your body is getting the support that it needs to be healthy. This can also reduce blood pressure.

**Detoxifies the Body and Mind**

A major part of the Reiki process is the removal of negative energies and toxins from your body. It cleanses the body and helps you naturally eliminate toxins that may have built up in your organs, digestive system, and bloodstream. You naturally encounter these toxins through your day—they are in some of the foods that you eat and the air that you breathe. Reiki also detoxifies the mind, clearing it of blockages that are stopping you from dealing with emotional trauma. This clearer state of mind and deeper understanding help you on the path to healing.

**Energizing and Rejuvenating**

Reiki is a very energizing practice. As you tap into your own spiritual energy and the connectedness between you and all that is in the Universe, you will feel your own energy grow. You will feel reinvigorated as the life force flows through your body. Some Reiki experts also say that the rejuvenation from Reiki has the ability to postpone that aging process and promote overall vitality.

Reiki is something that can take several attempts to get right. By knowing the benefits, you can be sure you are committing to a healing process. Reiki is worth learning, whether you use it to improve the quality of your own life or learn to transfer your energy to heal someone else.

# Chapter 3: How to Do Reiki on Yourself

Most people begin their journey of Reiki healing by practicing on themselves. It is necessary to start with yourself before healing others, as you must be physically and emotionally healed to be able to accept the healing energy of Reiki and channel it through your body. Though many people choose to take courses to ensure they are connecting to Reiki energy and using it to its full potential, it is possible to learn Reiki for beginners on your own. If you find yourself struggling, don't be afraid to look up tutorials or signup for a class nearby. This can help you take your Reiki connection and education to the next level.

## Step 1: Connecting with Reiki Energy

Creating with Reiki energy is about connecting with a heightened state of consciousness. In this state, you are aware of your connection to the life energy that flows through all the Universe. It should flow through effortlessly. Though connecting with Reiki energy is only the first step of practicing Reiki, it can be the most challenging for beginners. Do not become discouraged if you struggle with connecting to this heightened state, especially if you have not practiced any type of meditation before.

There are two parts to connecting to the Universal energy. First, you must speak to the Universe, let go of your ego, and open the connection to the wisdom and energy of the Universe. Once you are an open conduit for energy, you may use a visualization technique to feel the energy flowing through you.

### Reiki Invocation

When you enter the state of mind that allows you to connect to Reiki energy, you are connecting with the consciousness of Universal Energy. To do Reiki Invocation, it is as easy as speaking to this energy of the Universe and asking it for permission to conduct its energy as a healing channel. When you speak to the energy, you should have a calm and clear mind.

Beginners sometimes start their session with a few minutes of meditation to get them in the right frame of mind. Once you are relaxed, you will be able to speak to the Universal consciousness aloud or silently.

It does not necessarily matter how you ask to connect to this Universal Energy. You should choose to speak with the energy in a way that aligns with your own beliefs. However, the overall goal should be to pass on a pure form of healing and unconditional love. Once you have decided what to say and are ready to speak to the universe, place your palms together and position your hands in front of your heart chakra, as if in prayer. This is done using the heart chakra because healing must come from a place of love. The heart is the core of the emotions and the core of the soul. Once you are ready, you might say something like:

"I call upon the energy of the Universe and the energy of all the Reiki conduits of the past, present, and future to take part in this healing session. I call these energies near to me to create a stronger connection to the Universal energy.

I ask that these energies give me the infinite wisdom to channel this energy. I ask that the power of the Universal Energy flows through me and allows me to conduct unconditional love and pure healing, as well as grants me the knowledge to use and direct this energy where it is needed most.

I ask to be empowered through the blessings and divine love of the Universe."

It is important as you ask for this permission that you allow your shift to focus. You should not be focusing on yourself or your own ego being granted the ability to heal. Instead, you must raise your own consciousness and allow your questions to raise your vibrational energy. You must be in line with the Universal Energy so that the energy can flow through you as if you are a channel for its healing benefits.

Notice how as you speak to the universe, you are asking permission to be a conduit. You are not asking to be a healer or to make your own decisions in healing but are instead asking to be a conductor for the knowledge and wisdom of the universe. For this to be effective, you must allow your ego to float away and align your beliefs with the Universal consciousness, which is a higher state of knowledge and truth. As you settle into this greater power, you must let go of those beliefs that do not align with the laws of the Universe.

### *Visualizing Universal Energy Entering Your Palms*

The Universal Energy is not something that you can physically see, as it exists beyond a physical level of reality. This is the reason you must allow your mind to enter an altered state of consciousness to connect to it. Visualization can help you 'see' this connection beyond the realm of reality. As you bring that into your mind, you will physically feel the powerful energy of the Universe coursing through you. Here is an example of a visualization you may use:

Begin by closing your eyes and breathing in deeply. As you let go of this deep breath, see bluish-white energy beams as they surround you. These energy beams stretch from the ground, like threads connecting the grounds of the earth to the sky and beyond, connecting all that exists in the Universe.

As you become aware of these connections, feel yourself bathing in this light. Take another deep breath. As you release it, focus your energy on your palms, speaking to the Universal Energy around you. Breathe in the infinite light and call it into your palms, visualizing the light entering your body. As it flows through your body and out your palms, they glow with an energy that has a cool, white color. Now, you should be able to feel the Universal Energy radiating through your palms.

As you do the visualization technique, keep in mind that it does not matter what the energy looks like.

While visualizing it can help, you should sense or feel how the energy appears. Not everyone can physically see this energy, but that does not matter. It is your willpower and your willingness to connect to the Universal energy. It is your thoughts and willpower, as well as your willingness to be used as a conduit for the energy of the Universe, which creates the reality of your ability to heal.

## Step 2: Performing an Aura Scan

The way that people perceive the existence of auras is often incorrect. Your body does not create an aura or give off a type of visible energy. Rather, the aura describes a Universal energy. This energy surrounds all living things, but it is not really around it. A person's aura is not projected, as it exists within the body, too. The body is overlaid on the spiritual energy that is an aura.

Your aura is part of your energy system. It absorbs and puts off information, working much like the brain in the way that it is able to transmit and receive signals from the world. Everything that is inherently you exists within the aura, affecting its overall health. It is a collection of your vibration, as well as your memories, experiences, thoughts, and emotions. When you are experiencing a negative emotion, it can distort your aura and affect its health. For example, some negative thoughts may show up on your aura as a muddy, dark blob. Once it takes hold, this may present as a physical symptom.

Many people are aware that auras have different colors that transmit information about the mind and body. In addition to different colors, auras have properties including size, pattern, shape, and texture. The color also does not have to be solid, such as the case of certain textures or discolorations.

### Doing an Aura Scan on Yourself

Once you have connected with the Universal energy, you should feel the energy around you. Close your eyes to help with your visualization of this energy. Then, position your hands so they are just above your head, with your palms facing your body. You should either use your dominant hand or both of your hands for this exercise. Hold your hand(s) out in front of you, anywhere from 2-10" away from your body.

Starting above your head, you are going to move your hands down your body. If you would like, you can stop at the different energy points (chakras) along the body. Often, you can help yourself understand the specifics of imbalances or blemishes in your aura by paying attention to the different chakras of the body and what each area relates to. You'll learn more about the specifics of each chakra in the next chapter.

The first time that you move your hands down your body do a quick overall pass from your head to your hips. The base of the spine holds the root chakra, which is the lowest. Notice how you feel overall to gauge your energy. Then, do a second pass and be aware of the differences you might feel in different areas. Some areas may feel as if the energy is thicker or thinner, either speeding your hand along or slowing it down as you pass through. You may also sense subtle vibrations or temperature differences. If an area feels cooler, it means that the energy is flowing out. If it feels hotter, more energy is being drawn inward.

When you do notices differences, it is because your energy may need assistance or because it is in a state of change. This is when you move onto the next step using a targeted approach. You will have more success with aura scanning the more you practice. As you have more Reiki sessions, you will also find that you are more in tune with your body and what it needs for your energy to flow freely.

**Step 3: Setting Your Intention**

Setting your intention is as simple as stating what you want. By knowing what blockages or disruptions you are experiencing, you can trace this back to the root problem. By using a targeted approach and directing Reiki energy, you can heal specific ailments. Some examples of problems commonly healed during a Reiki session include:

- Achieving Spiritual Balance
- Reduction of Pain
- Reduced Stress
- Promote Healing of Trauma
- Promote Healing of Obesity
- Restoration of Relationships
- Improved Sleep
- Connect to a Higher Purpose
- Ability to Overcome Addiction
- Increased Positivity in Emotional State

You can think of your intention as a message. You are communicating to the aura, whether your own or another person's. This communication states your desired outcome and by directing your energy to that outcome, it strengthens the results. For your message to be heard, it must be clear and strong. As the Universe grants this request, the aura reflects that intention and heals the body and/or mind.

Setting your intention can be greatly improved by using Reiki techniques in combination with visualization. As you are focusing on your intention, visualize the outcome. Visualize how the outcome will change your life. Feel yourself becoming happier and focusing on more positive things, like going out dancing with your friends or having more time to spend with your significant other. Focus on the pain going away or on resolving whatever is holding you back.

For visualization to work, it must be incredibly vivid. Imagine how you would feel if your intention were to come true. Feel the relief of pain, whether emotional or physical. Imagine how you would look and feel if you were able to overcome your weight loss struggles or how refreshed and invigorated you would feel if you were able to get a full night of sleep. If you are healing someone else, visualize the changes that may come about and how they would feel if you were able to heal them. Combining visualization with setting your intention can have profound benefits and increase your Reiki healing power.

**Step 4: Activating Reiki Symbols**

Reiki symbols are symbols that you create with your hands that improve your ability to heal, transmit energy, and more. There are several symbols commonly used during Reiki, depending on your intended purpose and whether you are practicing on yourself or someone else.

To learn how to tap into Reiki power on a deeper level, it can be helpful to learn these symbols. While they will be described here, it would be impossible to describe how to do them in writing. You can find tutorials, charts, and other guides online that will help you with activating Reiki symbols the proper way. You could also take a class or speak with a Reiki teacher about learning these symbols. The most commonly used Reiki symbols include:

- Cho Ku Rei (Power Symbol)- The power symbol can amplify many things. It is commonly used at the beginning of a Reiki session to help amplify healing energy, as well as provide spiritual protection that people need when they are connecting to the aura of others to heal them. It may also be used to empower other symbols or infuse food with energy.

- Hon Sha Ze Sho Nen (Distance Symbol) - This symbol is about enlightenment, peace, and unification. As it unifies, healers typically use it when they are healing someone across a distance. It can also be used to send attunements across distances, allowing people to open their chakras and be receptive to the wholesome, healing energy of the Universe.

- Sei He Ki (Mental & Emotional Reiki Symbol) - This symbol is ideal when you are trying to heal yourself (or someone else) mentally or emotionally. It is attuned to the energies of love and wellbeing in the universe. Not only does it create a calmer mental state, but it may also be used to help someone release negative energies or remove addictions.

- Dai KO Myo (Master Symbol) - As the name suggests, the Master Symbol is the most powerful in Reiki. Often, it is only Reiki Masters that can connect with this symbol. It is used to create wondrous life changes, to heal the soul, and to relieve the body of disease and illness in the aura.

## Step 5: Guiding the Energy

One of the biggest mistakes that beginners in the world of Reiki healing make is believing that hand positions take priority over the other parts of the Reiki healing process. Things like being able to connect to the higher consciousness that allows you to access the energy of the Universe and setting your intention are much more important. However, it is possible to guide Reiki energy, especially when you are targeting a specific area of the body.

To direct Reiki energy, simply place your hands over the area you want to heal. Visualize and feel the energy flowing as you state your intention. If you are doing a full body Reiki session, then simply moving your hands over the body will be enough. As you guide the healing energy to the areas of your body that need it most, it is important to state your intention for each individual area you are trying to heal. Repeat steps 3-5 as many times as you need to before closing the connection. You will be finished when you can do an aura scan without feeling blockages or disruptions in energy.

**Step 6: Closing the Connection**

Another mistake that Reiki beginners often make is failing to close the connection between themselves and the Universe, or themselves and whoever they are trying to heal. When you fail to close the connection, you may absorb any negative energy that was released from your aura or the aura of the person you are trying to heal. If you do not close the connection, you can carry these emotions around and it may make you feel ill or exhausted.

The key to closing the connection is releasing any of the negative energies that have accumulated in your system. You can do this easily by visualizing all the negative energy flowing out of your body through your palms, releasing any negative energy that is stored in your system and leaving you in a rejuvenated state. As you connect with your typical energy, you will find yourself returning to your normal state of consciousness. Many people also wash their hands with cool water following a session to help them remove residual energies that may linger behind on the hands.

## Healing Others Using Reiki

Doing Reiki on others is a new way to conduct your healing energy. While there are slight differences from performing the healing ritual on yourself, you will notice some similarities in the actual healing process.

### *Doing an Aura Scan on Someone Else*

To do an aura scan on somebody else, you should begin by asking them to lie down. This will give you the best opportunity to sense their flow of energy through the different chakras. After you have opened your mind and body to the Universal Energy, visualize a white light that covers your body from head to toe. This white light will act as your shield, protecting you from absorbing any negative or unhealthy energy from the other person.

Use your dominant hand or both hands, as you would while sensing your own auras. Begin on the right side of the person's body and run your hands along the side, moving gradually but pausing for a few seconds at each chakra position (you can learn these positions in the next chapter). You will not need to hold your hands there as long after you get more practice. Make a mental note whenever you sense a disruption of the other person's aura. You will target this area later. If you cannot remember the area, keep a notebook and hand nearby and jot each area down. Then, do this with the left side of the body and make a mental note of any disruptions.

Now that you have done the initial scan place your hands over their body on problem areas, one at a time. Close your eyes as you place your hands over the block or negative energy and allow yourself to visualize the color, shape, size, and texture associated with the block. As you visualize the

106

blocks, you should feel yourself becoming familiar with what is causing the blocks. These details can point to someone's unhealthy behaviors, recurring mental patterns, and unresolved emotions. Before a person will be able to clear their head and allow life energy to flow through their body, it is critical that they review and solve these issues.

Something to keep in mind is that you should not have to strain yourself to hear these messages. If you cannot understand the meaning behind someone's block, do not worry. You will come to understand more and connect to the Universal consciousness in a deeper way as you continue to practice.

### Doing an Aura Scan across Distance

Some Reiki masters can heal across a distance, not only without physically touching someone but without the person being physically present. This healing is powerful and resonates through all the energy that makes up the world, forming a connection between the healer and the person they are trying to heal.

To begin healing across a distance, create a drawing on a sheet of paper. This should be a rough sketch of a body, though it does not have to resemble the person you are trying to scan. It is merely meant as a representation and reference sheet. Connect to Reiki energy as you would normally and visualize the white shield of light forming around you, protecting you from negative energies you may pick up while scanning your auras.

Begin by scanning using either your dominant hand or both hands. Scan the right side first, followed by the left, front, and back. You will do this by positioning your palm over different points on the sketch. If the connection is strong enough, you will experience a sensation of which areas of the body are blocked, much like you would if the person was lying in front of you. You should take note of these blocks and any messages that result. Then, you will use a blockage removal technique as you did before.

### Following Up

After the initial scan when you are working with someone else, you should talk to them about blockages or disruptions in their energy and what they could possibly mean. If you have received any messages from reading their aura, you should discuss them and point them out. While you may be able to heal someone's energy temporarily, the same blocks will resurface eventually unless the underlying problem is dealt with. Reiki can help with this, but other healing work may be necessary for total healing as well.

### Healing

Once you have followed up after the aura scan, you are ready to heal. You can conduct the healing the same way you would with yourself. You must set your intention, activate the Reiki symbols, and guide the energy. Finally, you will want to close the connection. This is even more important when healing others than when healing yourself since you will leave yourself open to the negativities you have just dispelled from their aura.

# Chapter 4: General Advice for Maximizing the Results of Your Reiki Session

The degree of healing that you experience after a Reiki session depends on several factors. The intensity of the session, your level of focus, and how open you are to the healing energy created during the session can all impact your effects. This chapter will provide some additional tips that can maximize the results of your Reiki healing session.

## Setting the Environment

One of the great things about Reiki is that it doesn't need any extra equipment or space, so you can practice it anywhere. While you should practice Reiki somewhere you can focus, it does not need to be absolutely silent for you to connect to the healing energies of the Universe. You may want to practice Reiki in your office building, for example, even as people hustle and bustle around you. As long as you can enter the right state of consciousness to connect to Reiki energy, you should not have any troubles. The goal is to choose an area where you can heal without resistance from your environment.

Many people also begin their Reiki session by washing their hands with cold water. Water is cleansing. It removes residual energy and purifies your immediate area. This will allow the healing energy of the Universe to flow freely from your hands, in its purest, most wholesome form.

## Mind-Body Alignment is Necessary

There is no practice that cannot make you do what you do not want to do. People who resist the idea of energy flow or who do not believe in the authenticity of new age topics will have trouble experiencing the results of a Reiki session. You must be open and receptive to the idea of Reiki alignment and be aware of the energy as it flows through you. Once you have opened your mind and are receptive to the energies, you will become aware of the way that energy feels as it courses through your body. It is then, and only then that you will be able to experience the benefits.

## Understanding Your Chakras

The chakras describe key energy points through the body. They have been studied for thousands of years, with the ancient texts called the Vedas detailing their abilities. The word 'chakra' translates to 'wheel' in Sanskrit, which makes sense as the chakras are considered the wheels of energy within the body. When the chakras are functioning well, they contribute to our existence and promote overall happiness and wellness in our lives. The chakra system is all about trying to achieve balance. When one chakra is under-active, or not active enough, other chakras may over-compensate. Each of the chakras governs a certain area or systems of the body. By understanding which areas of the body are affected by the chakras and paying attention to the messages received through aura scans, you can properly balance each area. This allows you to perform Reiki where it is needed most.

## Muladhara (Root Chakra)

The first of the chakras is the root chakra, which is sometimes considered the 'seat' of the soul since all the chakras sit upon this chakra and it channels the body's connection to the earth. The root chakra channels red light energy and it is located near your tailbone, between the base of your spine and belly button. It is common for the root chakra to become overactive since it is heavily used. When it is balanced, the root chakra makes you feel grounded. You should feel deeply rooted in your human experience. You should also feel a sense of peace and accomplishment when you think about your life in terms of safety, shelter, and money.

The root chakra affects your day-to-day life. For most people, the balance feels like financial and emotional security. When the root chakra is overactive, it can cause jitteriness and anxiety. This comes from a place of worry and fear, generally regarding one's survival. Anxiety problems can cause more than just jitteriness- it may cause lower back issues, digestive problems, hip pain, prostate problems in men, and ovarian cysts in women. An over-active root chakra may make you feel nervous, fearful, or unwelcome in your environment. When this chakra is over-active, it can also cause people to act greedy and materialistic. They may resist change and be obsessed with their overall sense of security. When the root chakra is under-active, which can happen when people have not struggled with their sense of security to life, it may cause them to be distant or 'spaced out.' People may describe them as not having their heads in the clouds.

You can encourage the balancing of this chakra by taking care of your survival needs. Otherwise, after being balanced, the chakra will act up again. However, you will find yourself with enough energy to do this after recharging the chakra. When you need to create calm in yourself, use the root chakra to focus on your connection to your spirit. People often care for this chakra by spending time in nature, connecting to spirit guides, meditating, or praying.

Acts of compassion and volunteering can also help, as kindness helps guide overactive energy away from the root chakra and power the other centers of the body.

### Svadhishana (Sacral Chakra)

The second chakra translates to 'the place of thy self.' The sacral chakra is the home of your creative energy. It is located just above the root chakra and just below the belly button, and the sacral chakra's orange, glowing power is connected to the human experience. The sacral chakra is also about pleasure, so when it is balanced, you will be able to enjoy the pleasures of life without overdoing them. This includes eating good food, having sex, and enjoying creative activities. These will nourish you and provide a sense of wellness and abundance.

If the second chakra is overactive, it can cause people to overindulge. This can cause problems like gluttony and addiction. A good sign that the chakra is over-stimulated is guilt that comes along with your pleasurable activities. You should not have to feel guilty about pleasure. Another cue of an imbalanced chakra system is trouble enjoying things that should be nourishing, like nutrient-dense, flavorful foods or sex with someone that you care about. Physically, problems with this chakra can cause hormone imbalances, addiction, restlessness, and obesity.

Ideally, you should balance the second chakra by consciously drawing the energy given to the pleasure center into the heart. It is easy to balance the sacral chakra, simply by asking yourself each time that you do something, "Is this activity good for me? Is it nourishing and healthy? What benefits could come from this activity?" As you assess your actions, you are taking the steps necessary to recognize those activities that do not suit your heightened consciousness and healthy existence. This gives you the insight needed to know when you need to draw energy from the sacral chakra and move it into the heart.

You may also need to balance this chakra by allowing energy to flow through it. When your sacral chakra is underactive, it may be indicative of you practicing things and working without having the time to enjoy yourself. This can cause problems like decreased sex drive, impotence, depression, and a lack of creativity and passion. When the chakra is underactive, you can energize it by making an effort to enjoy life. It can be hard to find time for pleasure when you lead a busy life, but it is important to do so if you want to avoid chakra imbalance.

### Manipura (Solar Plexus Chakra)

The Sanskrit for the third chakra translates to 'lustrous gem.' This is considered the gem of the soul, as it is where you create a sense of identity, self-confidence, and personal power. The solar plexus can be found just below the ribs, above the belly button and below the center of your chest. When it is balanced, you will have insight into life's situations and the wisdom to know when a situation is not right for you. You will also feel a sense of personal power in your life's situations, knowing that you are in control rather than feeling as if you are only along for the ride. The yellow energy from this chakra glows bright and is often called the warrior chakra, as it gives you the confidence to excel and the wisdom to be familiar enough with your personal truth that you know what you are fighting for.

When the solar plexus chakra is out of overactive, it becomes apparent in the way that the power we have over our own lives begins to spill over into the lives of other people. This creates a desire to micromanage others and exercise total control. It can also make you greedy, quick to anger, and lacking in empathy and compassion. Physically, this can cause digestive issues and imbalances of the internal organs, including the kidney, liver, pancreas, and appendix. To bring about balance, you can open your heart and focus on compassion and love. Meditate and focus your intention on projecting love and kindness the people around you. Rather than allowing your chakra to focus on your own needs, visualize yourself as a beacon of love.

The solar plexus may become blocked when our ability to control our own life's circumstances are taken away. This can make you feel indecisive, needy, timid, and insecure. To reconnect and reenergize the third chakra, spend time reflecting on your abilities and talents. Everyone has something they are good at. Now, make a list of all the things you would say you are 'good' at. You do not have to be especially talented at them—it's okay if you are an artist, but not Picasso. Empower yourself by creating affirmations and reflecting on those things that give you empowerment and make you the person you are.

### Anahata (Heart Chakra)

The Sanskrit for Anahata translates to 'unhurt.' The heart chakra is associated with green energy and it is known as the center of love, empathy, kindness, and compassion. This includes not only the love you hold for others but the love you have for yourself. It is located near the center of your chest, between the throat and breastbone.

When the heart chakra is balanced, you will find yourself feeling love equally for yourself and others. This allows you to meet your commitments while leaving yourself time for the self-care you need. Additionally, when you or someone else goes through troubles, you can still see the kindness and compassion that radiates from within them.

When the heart chakra is overactive, it can cause you to make unhealthy choices. You forget personal boundaries and are driven by your desire to love. Often, this presents as finding yourself putting the needs of others before yourself. However, it is important to remember that you cannot pour from an empty cup and you must also find time to love yourself. Treat yourself with the same level of kindness, forgiveness, and compassion that you would treat others. Physically, an overactive heart chakra can cause intense heartburn, problems with interpersonal relationships, heart palpitations, and a fast heart rate. The key to balancing your heart chakra is finding the time that you need for yourself.

Commit to doing something for yourself at least once per day. You could do a self-massage (or have someone do it for you), take a relaxing bath, or do something that you truly enjoy. As you set your intention and meditate, you should focus on sending yourself the compassion that you give so selflessly to others.

If the heart chakra is underactive, it can cause problems of the heart. This sometimes happens as a result of heartbreak and other harsh lessons of the world. When you cannot stop yourself from taking these lessons of life personally, it can cause your heart chakra to be blocked. This could be compared to building a wall around your heart, causing you to struggle to get close to others and to share pieces of yourself. This presents physically as circulation problems and the feeling that you are not present in your body. You may go through life on autopilot, simply living your life without any emotional attachment. As most people work hard to build the defenses around their heart, it can be hard to knock them down as well. You should start with self-care to energize your heart chakra. As you find yourself able to project love and compassion on yourself, begin to project on the world around you again.

### Vishuddha (Throat Chakra)

Vishuddha translates to 'very pure' which relates to the chakra's ability to reveal and connect to your personal traits. It is the center of communication and allows you to speak your truth with clarity. It is located right above the heart and has a bright blue energy. When you are balanced, you find yourself with the knowledge to decide which words are appropriate for the situation. While you will speak clearly with truth, love, and kindness, you will also have the enlightenment to speak out against things that are unkind or unjust. Having a balanced throat chakra can also create inspiration and enlightenment for those around you.

The fifth chakra often becomes overactive when we struggle with having our voice heard for some reason, usually accompanied by feelings of being invalidated or ignored. As you do not feel like you are being heard, the throat chakra can cause you to interrupt others, speak loudly, or simply talk a lot. Physically, people who struggle with an overactive throat chakra may suffer from mouth ulcers, cavities, frequent infections, and throat pain. To bring about balance to an overactive throat chakra, you must get in the habit of thinking before you speak. Instead of blurting the first thing that comes to mind, ask if what you are saying is true, necessary, and kind. If so, then you should continue to speak.

Over time, failing to speak your personal truth can cause you to shut down. People may refer to you as quiet or shy and you may find yourself unable to express what you are feeling to others, even in times of crisis or upset. It is not uncommon for digestive issues to result from an underactive throat chakra, since the emotions may be swallowed down instead of being set free. The best way to start energizing this throat chakra is to practice speaking about your feelings and your personal truths. Even allowing your own ear to receive these truths can help give your chakra the energy it needs.

### Anja (Third Eye Chakra)

This chakra, translating to "beyond wisdom," opens your mind in a way that you can perceive the world beyond your five natural senses. For some people, this presents only as an intuition. For others, a balanced third eye chakra can result in psychic energy or extrasensory perception. The third eye chakra is associated with the color deep purple or indigo and is located between the eyes, deep inside the forehead. The pineal gland of the brain is said to represent the third eye chakra. This is a small, pinecone-shaped gland that regulates your sleep and wake schedule.

The third eye chakra is balanced when you feel equally in tune with the spiritual and physical world. While you will receive information from something outside of your normal five senses, this emotion should not be presented in a way that overwhelms you. The third eye is heavily celebrated in many cultures, with the Ancient Egyptians, Indians, and other cultures recognizing its properties long before technology allowed brain scans to detect the pineal gland.

Aside from people who are heavily attracted to paranormal experiences, astrology, tarot card readings, and the like, it is difficult for the third eye to be over stimulated. Most people experience the opposite, as fluoride that is commonly found in water and other sources tends to accumulate on the pineal gland and affect third eye abilities. However, when people do experience an overactive third eye, as well as those who have psychic powers, may be overwhelmed by their insight from the world. It can become distracting and take away from the physical human experience. If you do find yourself distracted from the human experience, take some time being a human. Go to the beach and immerse your toes in the sand or stick your feet in a stream in the woods. Immerse yourself in the experience, stating, "I am a human being. I am a human doing".

The world that we live in typically invalidates the development of intuition and psychic abilities, as those things that cannot be physically seen or proven with science are often said not to exist. For this reason, people are more likely to have an underactive third eye chakra than an overactive one. When your third eye chakra is underactive, it can cause you to disconnect from spiritual experiences. Some common problems that result include allergies, sinus troubles, and headaches. Meditation is the best way to energize the sixth chakra. First focus on the signals outside your body, then spend time listening to your spirit and realizing its place in the world. As you continue to practice, connecting with the third eye will become easier.

### *Sahaswara (Crown Chakra)*

The final chakra is the seventh chakra, which is located just above the head. It has an energy unlike any of the other chakras, as it connects us to the entire Universe. One way to think of it is a seed of conscious energy that rests above your head, encouraging your connection to all that is around you. The crown chakra is associated with a violet and white energy. When it is balanced, you may feel as if you are a spiritual warrior. While most people do not reach the state of perfect balance in their lifetime, as it is similar to the Buddhist concept of Nirvana. It is the overcoming of suffering and death when the soul has achieved its highest state of ascension. However, it is not necessarily achieving this that creates balance with the crown chakra, as most people take several lifetimes or longer to conquer their ascension. It is the journey of achieving this balance and moving upward. It is the journey and the progression that brings wisdom, good health, and happiness.

It is not possible for the crown chakra to be overactive, as it is connected to the energy of the Universe. It is impossible to exist in the physical world and be overcome with energy from consciousness, so it is not important to balance. However, the crown chakra is commonly underactive. Most people have an underactive crown chakra, as it feels exactly like a human experience. You can raise the energies of your seventh chakra by balancing your other chakras and practicing spiritual development. Doing things like meditating and connecting with the consciousness will invigorate your crown chakra. Be sure to focus on all the chakras and not just the crown chakra, as the crown chakra cannot be stimulated unless all the other chakras are in balance.

## Breathing in Reiki Energy

One technique that you can use to amplify your Reiki energy is to breathe it and imagine the life force filling you. Close your eyes and deeply breathe through your nose, deep enough that if there were someone sitting next to you, they would audibly hear your breath sounds. As you inhale, feel the energy of life filling you with breath. Feel the energy as your chest and stomach expand, filling you up with breath.

Now, as you exhale, feel your body becoming soft. As the breath leaves you, everything relaxes. If you have trouble connecting to Reiki energy, preparing in this way lets you connect to Reiki energy and feel the life force. It is most useful before you use visualization to imagine the force of the Universe flowing inside of you.

# Chapter 5: Advancing Your Reiki Practice

You should always begin your Reiki practice by doing sessions on yourself. Once you are confident in healing yourself, if you have the desire to, you can also learn to heal the flow of energies through other people. It is generally advised once you are ready to advance your practice that you learn from a professional. However, this chapter will guide you through the basics.

## The Three Degrees of Reiki

Reiki practice is something that has different levels, with the lowest level being reserved for people who want to practice Reiki on themselves and the highest level being reserved for people who learn from and become Reiki masters.

### *First Degree Reiki*

First Degree Reiki is the main focus of this book. This involves self-care and is training that allows you to practice Reiki in daily life. Many people trained in First Degree Reiki can also place their hands on family and friends to promote Reiki healing. It is not uncommon for people in the healthcare field to learn First Degree Reiki, as it can be used as a complementary medicine. Usually, massage therapists, nurses, and other people who are in a profession where it is appropriate to touch patients will study First Degree Reiki.

### Second Degree Reiki

Second Degree Reiki is practiced across a distance. It is ideal for situations where touch might not be possible or when it is inappropriate, such as in the case of psychotherapists who may want to learn Reiki to help patients to process emotional trauma. Second Degree Reiki relies on creating a mental connection, rather than a hands-on approach. In other situations, the mental connection may be established to enhance the effects of the Reiki session and promote a greater flow of energy.

### *Third Degree Reiki*

Third Degree Reiki is the highest level, being achieved only by Reiki masters. To officially earn certification as a Reiki master, it is generally accepted that you must receive an invitation from an existing Reiki master. The people who are extended this invitation are those who have devoted their lives to the practice of Reiki and teaching it to others. Since it requires an invitation from a Reiki master, Third Degree Reiki is generally learned through a long apprenticeship.

### **Reiki Attunement**

A major component of practicing Reiki is the vibrational frequencies. You can only channel the healing energies of the Universe that you have been attuned to. It is not uncommon for a Reiki attunement to be performed before someone moves up to the next degree of Reiki since increasing your vibrational frequency will give you the opportunity to increase your healing potential.

A Reiki attunement can be done by a Reiki teacher who possesses the ability to open your chakras in a way that allows a higher state of consciousness to flow through you. To have the ability to make your energy flow through someone else, these chakras must be able to put forth and absorb energy, connecting you to the flow of life energy in the universe and allowing you to channel it through someone else's body. The process of Reiki attunement may also be called expanding your energy channels. If you do not want to work with a Reiki teacher, then you may also be able to raise your vibrational frequency by doing Chi exercises, which will be discussed next.

Alternatively, you can work on balancing and then energizing each of your chakras on your own. While this may take longer and require a greater deal of focus than when working with a Reiki master, it is a great alternative if you do not have access to a Reiki instructor. Below, you'll find guidelines for opening each of the chakras. As you read the chants, keep in mind that 'A' is pronounced 'ah' when chanting and 'M' is pronounced like 'mng,' as if it has an 'ng' like the word thing.

- Crown Chakra- To open the crown chakra, place your hands in front of your stomach. Allow the ring fingers to point upward and touch at the tips before crossing the other fingers, ending with the left thumb being positioned under the right. Once your hands are in position, begin to focus on the crown chakra. You may visualize this as a white or purple light above the head if you would like. Then, chant the sound NG. As a note, you should not use this to open the crown chakra unless you have a solid foundation upon the root chakra.
- Third Eye Chakra- Sit somewhere you are comfortable and bring your hands to the lower part of your chest. Place your hands so the middle fingers are straightened, with each touching at the tip and pointing forward.

Then, bend the other fingers so that they touch near the top at the second joint. Allow the thumbs to touch as well, pointing toward your body. Now, focus on the third eye where it is located above the eyebrows. As you visualize its indigo energy, chant the sound AUM.

- Throat Chakra- To open the throat chakra, position your hands so your fingers overlap each other on the inside. Allow the thumbs to touch near the top, then pull them up slightly so they stick out. You may position your hands near your chest. Focus on the blue energy of the throat chakra, which is located at the base of the throat. While you do this, chant the sound associated with this chakra— HAM.

- Heart Chakra- You should begin opening the heart chakra by sitting in a cross-legged position. Bring your index finger and thumb together to form a circle. Then, place your right hand just above your solar plexus and place the left hand on the left knee. Focus on the green, glowing energy of the heart chakra, right near your chest. The sound associated with this chakra is YAM.

- Navel Chakra- To open the navel chakra, position your hands on the area just below your ribcage and above your stomach. Let your fingers join together, palms against each other with the fingers pointing directly outward. Let the thumbs cross and be sure the fingers are straight. Now, focus on the area above the navel and see it as a ball of glowing yellow energy. As you visualize this energy and feel it course through you, chant the sound RAM.

- Sacral Chakra- You should open the sacral chakra while in a sitting position. Place your hands in your lap with the palms facing skyward. Let them overlap, with the left hand on the bottom and its palm touching the back of your fingers on your right hand. Once your hands are in position, allow the tips of the thumbs to come together. Now, focus on the energy in your lower back and navel, imagining it as a glowing orange ball of energy. When you are ready, begin chanting VAM.

- Root Chakra- Open the root chakra by bringing your thumb and index finger together at the tip, so they form a circle. Focus on the root chakra, imagining a glowing red ball of energy if you would like. As you feel the power of the root chakra, chant the sound LAM.

Before you settle into a chant to open one of your chakras, be sure that you are relaxed. It is best to fall into a meditative state of mind beforehand. This will give you the focus and attention that you need to bring about change with your chanting.

# Chapter 6: Additional Therapies to Use with Reiki

Often, Reiki is not used as a standalone therapy. While it can produce results on its own, especially when it is performed by someone that has earned the title of Reiki Master, there are additional therapies that can be used to increase the results of Reiki healing. This chapter will go over some of them so that you can get the most of your Reiki healing sessions.

## Crystal Therapy

Crystals are made up of elements of the earth. They carry a unique vibrational energy depending on what they are made out of. This vibrational energy allows them to attune to your body, producing certain effects. It is not uncommon for people to wear certain stones or carry them around. They can also be used during Reiki and other practices, as a way to enhance the results.

To add crystals to your Reiki session, you can put your hands into position over the chakras as you focus your intention and your healing energy. Hold the appropriate crystal in your hand and channel the energy into yourself or the person you are healing. The crystal that you use depends on which chakra you are trying to heal, excite, or calm. You can choose whichever crystal has the strongest pull or seems to call to you, or you can choose one that goes with the specific chakra you are trying to heal. Here are some of the crystals that should be used for each of the chakras:

- Crown Chakra- Clear Quartz, Diamond, Ametrine, Clear Calcite, Amethyst/Violet
- Third Eye Chakra- Lazuli, Lapis/Indigo, Quartz, Sodalite
- Throat Chakra- Turquoise/Blue, Celestite, Blue Lace Agate, Aquamarine
- Heart Chakra- Pink Calcite, Emerald/Green, Rose Quartz, Tourmaline

- Solar Plexus Chakra- Amber/Yellow, Malachite, Aragonite, Moonstone, Topaz
- Sacral Chakra- Carnelian, Orange Stones, Smoky Quartz, Red Jasper
- Root Chakra- Lodestone/Red, Bloodstone, Tiger's Eye, Ruby, Garnet, Hematite

Something to keep in mind is that crystals can take on negative energy as people would. Some people choose to release negative energy on their crystal by performing a Reiki session to clean the crystal's aura before their own. There are several other options, including burning sage to cleanse the crystal or soaking it in saltwater. Some people also bury their crystals in salt, especially if they are soft and will be harmed by a saltwater bath. To amplify the power of a crystal, you can stick it on a windowsill or in direct moonlight. This works best when the moon is highly visible.

## Pray or Meditate

Many people stay away from the prayer option because they believe they must claim a religion or choose a specific God if they are to pray. However, prayer does not have to be directed at anyone or anything specific. If you are not comfortable praying, you could also meditate.

This is a time when you should focus on your intentions. Get in the habit of focusing on the positives of what you want. Instead of saying that you do not want pain, say that you want to heal. Even when you say something negatively, by reflecting on it as you meditate, you are giving it your focus and energy. This can draw that thing into your life or cancel out what you are trying to achieve with the prayer.

You should always look at meditation and prayer as an opportunity to reflect and look inward. Even if you are speaking outward, whether to your God, the Universe, or whatever you believe in, it is important to look inward. Speaking out loud can help trigger insights that you may not have realized otherwise.

It does not matter how long you pray or when you pray. Simply set aside time each day, whether a few minutes or longer. Make it a habit. If you can, speak out loud as you pray and really focus on the things that you need to be happy in your life.

**Yoga**

Yoga originally comes from India, however, it has recently become popular around the world. It is used for physical activity but also encourages the development of a more spiritual mindset. The type of yoga that you participate in has a lot to do with the effects, as the positions and breathing patterns have the ability to invoke certain results.

As you do yoga, you should always use the breathing practice called 'Pranayama.' This type of breathing is necessary for people who are trying to bring results to their yoga session. It allows you to connect with the Universe, while improving your physical and mental strength, increasing your memory power, and even extending your lifespan. You can take a class for yoga. Alternatively, look up positions or videos online. You'd be surprised how much information is available once you know where to look!

## Serve Others

We may do the things that our family, friends, and co-workers ask us regularly. However, fewer people take time out of their busy weeks to help those who truly need it. The reality is that every person is fighting a battle that nobody else understands. For example, someone who is homeless is not necessarily lazy—they are the result of a collection of life circumstances that could just as easily happen to you or me.

As you start to explore the world and help the people that truly need it, you will find yourself better prepared to help others. You will find a newfound sense of satisfaction in yourself and the responsibilities of life, as you realize that you can be responsible for more than just your normal day-to-day routine. As a person that connects to the Universe, you have the knowledge and wisdom to help those around you. Additionally, helping those who are less fortunate gives you the opportunity to gain your own maturity, strength, and knowledge when it comes to fighting battles in your life.

## Nourish Your Soul

Nourishing the soul is all about learning those things that make you happy and bring you peace—and then making an effort to do them. When you work long hours or have a hectic family life, it is hard to find time for yourself. It is important to remember that you owe yourself this nourishment. It is necessary for you to take care of yourself if you want to connect to the Universal consciousness and connect with others.

In addition to nourishing yourself by committing time to yourself, it is essential that you take care of your physical body and mind. Be sure that you get enough sleep each night. Practice relaxation techniques if you need to. You should also choose nutrient-dense foods, rather than those that are filled with empty calories. By nourishing your body and mind, you will find yourself in the best possible state to encourage mental, emotional, and spiritual healing and wellness too.

## Be Mindful in Your Experience

People lead busy lives. As you rush from task to task, when do you make time to slow down? Think back to the last time that you had a meal. Were you rushing to get back to whatever task you were doing before or even checking your emails while you ate? What about your last trip to the store or to work? Did you look around you as you went and observe the sights, or were you on autopilot mode as you just tried to get from A to B?

It is easy to become so immersed with the physical experience that we forget to slow down and experience the world in all its beauty. Instead of going on autopilot, make an effort to notice the things you are doing. When you are washing dishes or sweeping the floor, pay attention to the way the muscles move in your arms, shoulders, and back. As you eat, pay attention to the different flavors and textures you are getting from the food. Immerse yourself in the experience of eating and chew slowly enough that you can take it all in. Whenever you are driving or walking, notice your surroundings. Instead of staring at the carpet when you are rushing to your office in the morning, make an effort to smile at your coworkers. It doesn't take any extra time to move the muscles in your face. By immersing yourself in your human experience, you will find yourself more connected to your spiritual one as well.

# Conclusion

Reiki healing allows you to connect with the energies of the Universe and use it in a way that encourages the body to heal itself. It can be used to treat aches and pains, overcome allergies and headaches, and even heal chronic or painful diseases. The results depend heavily on your abilities and your mindset, as it is important to be receptive to the Reiki energies for them to result.

Often, the emotional and physical health problems that we struggle with stem from blocked energy channels in the body. Energy channels can be blocked after certain life circumstances or from being neglected. As you learn to encourage the flow of Universal energy through your body, you can promote overall health and wellness. You can stop at learning to heal yourself or you can continue our practice to strengthen your abilities and possibly heal others.

Hopefully, this book has been able to help provide the foundation for Reiki knowledge that you can build upon later. For the time being, however, you should know what you need to put your Reiki skills to work. The only thing left to do is practice! Your abilities will strengthen with time and as you become more aware of the way that the energies of the universe and your body affect you.

Best of luck!

# References

https://www.holisticshop.co.uk/articles/guide-reiki-healing

https://reiki-bangalore.com/all-about-reiki.shtml

http://healthmantra.com/reiki/reiki_notes.shtml

https://reiki-bangalore.com/why-reiki.shtml

https://www.livescience.com/40275-reiki.html

https://www.reiki.org/faq/HistoryOfReiki.html

https://www.reiki-for-holistic-health.com/

https://www.chakra-anatomy.com/benefits-of-reiki.html

https://www.takingcharge.csh.umn.edu/can-i-learn-reiki-myself

https://www.reikiinfinitehealer.com/lifeforce-energy-optimization

http://www.threshold.ca/reiki/Using-Reiki-To-Scan-Yourself.html

https://reikirays.com/12467/how-to-do-an-aura-scan-in-person-distance-scanning/

file:///C:/Users/saman/Downloads/ultimate-guide-connecting-reiki-energy.pdf

https://blog.mindvalley.com/7-chakras/

https://www.eclecticenergies.com/chakras/open

https://reikirays.com/16881/crystals-reiki-a-basic-guide/

https://spiritualray.com/spiritual-growth-exercises

https://www.powerofpositivity.com/7-exercises-for-spiritual-strength/

# Introduction: Understanding Crystals, their Healing Powers, and a Brief History

Crystals are formed under the surface of the earth over millennia. Crystals and gemstones are special rocks because the molecular structure within these rocks has repetitive patterns. The repetitive molecular patterns are formed depending on the heat, pressure, vibrational and other forms of energy these substances were subjected to over millions of years.

Therefore, it is right to assume that crystals have millennia-old universal energy trapped within them that can effectively be harnessed for healing and other purposes today. Crystals and gemstones have fascinated humankind from the beginning of time, and this intense fascination could be a result of one or more of the following reasons:

- Crystals are beautiful to look at. They dazzle in the sunlight, and the myriad colors of nature that they emanate can grab and hold anyone's attention.
- From ancient times, human beings have believed and leveraged the healing powers of these crystals.

- Crystals are flexible and dynamic and can be easily included into your spiritual enhancement regimen.

Healing with crystals and gemstones is not a new phenomenon. They have always been used by humankind since time immemorial. Amulets and talismans have always found a place in the history of human beings. Let us take a brief historical journey into the use of crystals for their healing and spiritually uplifting powers.

## A Brief History of Crystals and Gemstones

Excavations in Singur, Russia have unearthed mammoth ivory beads that are believed to be more than 60,000 years old. Amulets made of Baltic amber that are considered to be over 30,000 years old, and amber beads over 10,000 years old have been excavated in certain parts of Britain.

Excavations of the graves of the Paleolithic Age (in present-day Belgium and Switzerland) threw up necklaces, bracelets and beads made from crystals. The Sinai Peninsular in Egypt has been the home of malachite mines for 4000 years ago.

The first recorded history of the use of crystals is from the Ancient Sumerian Civilization who used crystals and gemstones to create magic formulas and potions. The Ancient Egyptians were not far behind, and they wore clear quartz, emerald, turquoise and lapis lazuli as jewelry for health and protection purposes.

The Ancient Greeks also attributed multiple properties to many crystals and, in fact, many of the crystal names have their roots in the ancient Greek language. The word, 'crystal' itself means 'ice' in the Greek language because the ancient Greeks believed that water solidified and froze at such depths and under such tremendous pressure that it became permanently crystallized and could not revert to its former liquid state. Amethyst means 'not drunk' and was used to prevent hangovers and drunkenness.

Interestingly, some crystals were believed to have similar medicinal and healing properties by different and disparate civilizations separated by thousands of miles. For example, Jade was believed to have kidney-healing properties by the Chinese, the Mayan, and the Aztec Civilizations. Turquoise is worn for health and vitality and jasper calmness and health the world over.

Then, in the Middle Ages, crystals were banned by the church for various reasons. During the Renaissance periods, the probing intellectuals started looking for scientific reasons for the behavior and properties of crystals. Now, of course, crystals are not used extensively in the mainstream medical industry, but they continue to be used by believers for mental and physical healing and health.

## Why and How Do Crystals Work?

Marcel Vogel was one of the first scientists who did some pioneering experiments with crystals and their healing powers. While he observed the growth of crystals under a microscope, he noticed that they took the form or the shape of whatever he was thinking about.

Based on these interesting and strange observations, Marcel Vogel postulated that the bonds between the molecules in the crystals had the power to continually assemble and reassemble to align with the thoughts and the mind of the observer. Further, he studied and tested the metaphysical power latent in the quartz crystal and concluded that it can store thoughts just like magnetic tapes record and store sound.

Albert Einstein believed that all things in the universe are composed of vibrational energy. These vibrational energies behave like sound waves in such a way that your thoughts align with everything else in your life, and vice versa. Therefore, the vibrational energies in the crystal have the power to amplify your thoughts.

Thoughts create vibrations in the universe, and therefore setting the right intention with your thoughts is a powerful tool to achieve happiness and well-being. A clear intention, goal, or purpose helps us identify with and understand our deepest desires and dreams. Additionally, focusing on thoughts to create the right intention increases our self-awareness and facilitates living 'in the moment.'

Intentions behave like magnets attracting resources and other elements in the universe that help in making our dreams a reality. Here are some tips on how to set intentions before you start working with crystals:

***Decide what is important to you*** - Your values and intentions are the driving force in your life. In the absence of intentions and values, your life is bound to move haphazardly, and you will not find fulfillment. Therefore, take some time off from your hectic routine, and think about the things that matter to you the most.

***Ask yourself which areas of your life need improvement*** – What aspects of your life need improvement? Are relationships an issue? Do you want to improve your health, spirituality, community and social life, career, or anything else?

***Create specific intentions and goals*** – Decide what you want to achieve, when, and how. Also, identify the reason behind your intentions. Why do you want to do what you want to do?

***Now, give life to your intentions*** – Some of the rituals using crystals require you to write down your intentions as if they are happening right now in your life. Fill your intentions with powerful emotions and feelings, and fill your mind with thoughts of your goals and intentions.

Certain crystals amplify these intentions, and by the law of attraction, you will be able to draw the required resources and energies from the universe to make your intentions become a reality.

Here is another way crystals work for our benefit. Our thoughts fill our minds preventing us from connecting with the universal energies that surround us. Crystals help in silencing our thoughts so that we can reconnect with the universal energy and feel rejuvenated and refreshed. Another critical lesson taught by crystals is patience. It took eons for crystals to trap the power of the earth and universe within their molecular systems. In the same way, we need to be patient and persist in our efforts to harness the healing powers of crystals.

Therefore, as you begin your journey to the wonderful world of crystals and their healing powers, remember to persist and be patient with yourself and the world around you. With practice, your ability to harness the healing power of crystals will improve slowly but surely.

# Chapter One: Choosing the Right Crystals for You

Experts in the crystal world believe that you don't choose the crystal. The crystal chooses you. Yet, there is plenty of information and experience that has been passed through generations of believers of the power of crystal that it does make sense to learn as much as you can before taking your first step into this magical and mesmerizing world.

If you are choosing a crystal from a bricks-and-mortar store, all you need to do initially is to walk around the shop and look at all the crystals on display. It is highly likely that one or two stand out in your eyes, and you might really not be able to pinpoint a tangible reason for this phenomenon at that point in time. And yet, there will be a 'calling,' for want of a better word, where these 1-2 crystals appear almost as if they are trying to reach out to you. This is what crystal experts believe happens with all crystal choices.

Here are some general guidelines that could, perhaps, give you some insight into the 'process' that goes into making the right crystal choice.

## Seek Help from the Universe

Yes, when you desire something deeply enough, the entire universe aligns with your desire and gives you multiple signs to help you in your search. Here are some tips to recognize signs sent by the universe:

*Request for signs* – Human beings are creatures of a powerful free will and the ability to think and visualize our needs. The spiritual capability inherent in each of us can recognize and receive guidance from the universe. You can ask for signs by making a little note of your request in your journal requesting signs. It could be something as simple as a thought that sparks in your mind or a simple prayer that comes to your lips. These are all powerful signs.

*Become familiar with various ways that the universe connects with you* – The language of the universe is different from that which you speak with your friends and family. The universal energy uses different ways to connect with you. It could be in the form of animals or numbers or colors or words from a wise elder in your home or even dreams that keep coming up in your life trying to tell you something. These are signs from the universe. Be sensitive to them, and familiarize yourself with them.

***Acknowledge, accept, and act on these signs***
– When you acknowledge a sign that has been sent to you, the universe understands that you are now open and alert to receiving more such messages. Therefore, instead of ignoring these signs, acknowledge, accept and act on them with your body, mind and soul. The more you recognize and acknowledge signs transmitted to you, the more the universe can connect with you.

## Seek Out Any Physical Reactions with Any Crystal

Take your non-dominant hand and pass it over different crystals. Sometimes, if the vibrational energy between your thoughts and the energy of the crystals resonate, then you could feel a 'tug' on your hand or palm. They are subtle but unmistakably physical reactions. Check out for such physical reactions to choose your crystal(s).

## Identify the Crystal or Gemstone for Your Particular Problem

As a beginner, this could, perhaps, be your first option. What is the problem that you are trying to solve? Pick up a crystal, which is empowered with the property to solve this particular problem.

A good place to begin this learning is by understanding which part of your body needs healing. Each part of the body is identified with chakras or wheels of energy, and the vibrational energy of each chakra is aligned with the energy of certain crystals. Therefore, you can choose the crystal based on the chakra that needs healing.

## Chakras and Their Significance to Our Well-Being

At this juncture, it makes sense to spend some time on the various chakras in the body, their energy purpose, and their corresponding crystals. Chakras with blocked energies or other functional problems can result in illnesses of the body and mind. Therefore, understanding each chakra, its position, and significance is important for healing. There are seven primary chakras in our body including:

*The root chakra* – Located at the base of your backbone in the region of the tailbone, the root chakra represents your grounding and foundational strength. The root chakra is responsible for survival issues such as finances, food, money, etc. It is associated with the color red.

A low level of energy in this chakra results in fearfulness and lack of self-confidence. Emotional and physical stability could also be hampered. An excessive amount of energy in the root chakra could result in an excessive feeling of attachment in a negative way such as clinging on to old and valueless belief systems that are hampering your physical, mental and intellectual growth.

Typically, red-colored crystals such as red jasper, hematite, smoky quartz, etc. help in healing and balancing the root chakra.

*The sacral chakra* – This chakra is situated in the lower abdomen about 2 inches below your navel and 2 inches inside. It is connected to your sexual and relationship energy. A healthy and balanced sacral chakra helps you maintain strong connections with others and facilitates new experiences with new situations and people. The sacral chakra is associated with wellbeing, plenitude, sexuality, and pleasure.

When the energy levels in the sacral chakra are lower than needed, then you could feel emotionally stifled and sexually inactive. You could disconnect with people around you. On the other hand, an overactive sacral chakra could lead to mood disorders such as bipolarity, depression, anxiety, etc.

The sacral chakra is connected to the color, and the crystals that can help in its healing are coral and orange calcite, orange carnelian, citrine, and orange aventurine.

***The solar plexus chakra*** – Located in the upper abdomen, this chakra's energy represents your self-confidence. It reflects your ability to control your life. The emotional issues controlled by the solar plexus chakra include self-esteem and self-confidence.

A lower-than-needed energy level in this chakra could result in a feeling of low self-esteem, a feeling of being invisible, and not allowing your personal power to be active. An overactive solar plexus chakra could result in a domineering, compulsive, and obsessive personality.

Yellow is the color of the solar plexus chakra. The crystals that help to heal and balance this chakra are pyrite stones (that hold the power of the golden sun), golden Lemurian, agate stone, and tiger's eye.

***The heart chakra*** – The energy of the heart chakra reflects your ability to give and receive love. It is located just above the heart in the center of the chest. It deals with inner peace, love, and joy. The heart chakra helps you to feel; an important element needed for all kinds of healing. A healthy and balanced heart chakra radiates love for yourself and for others around you.

A blocked or imbalanced heart chakra will make feel detached from the world around you, from people who love and care for you, and even from self-love. This chakra is associated with the color green. Crystals of the heart chakra include aventurine, amazonite, jade, malachite, and rose quartz.

**_The throat chakra_** – Located at the throat, this chakra reflects our communication ability. It deals with expressions of feelings and articulation. It also represents the expression of truth.

An imbalanced throat chakra results in compromised communication capabilities. You will find yourself unable to express your emotions and feelings. You will feel trapped. The color of the throat chakra is blue.

Crystals that promise to heal the throat chakra include sodalite, Angelite, lapis lazuli, aquamarine, azurite, and turquoise.

**_The third eye chakra_** – Located between the eyes on the forehead, the third eye chakra reflects our ability for focus and concentrate and helps us to see the bigger picture. It is associated with imagination, intuition, wisdom, extrasensory perceptions, and our ability to think through various things and take appropriate decisions.

A balanced and healthy third eye chakra helps you depend on your inner senses and intuition for guidance in various decision-making aspects of your life. The third eye chakra helps you include the powers of your soul along with your intellect and emotions to make beneficial decisions. A blocked third eye chakra could make you feel fearful and uncertain about the future of your life.

The color of the third eye chakra is purple. Crystals that are useful for healing this chakra include fluorite, shungite, amethyst, lapis lazuli, and quartz.

***The crown chakra*** – Located at the top of your head, the crown chakra is associated with your spiritual ability. It deals with balancing the outer and inner beauty of the body and mind, and your relationship with spirituality, inner consciousness and bliss.

A balanced and healthy crown chakra represents your desire to enhance yourselves spiritually. It reflects in your ability to empathize and a deep connection with the Supreme Being. An unbalanced or blocked crown chakra could result in your inability to reach out for higher wisdom resulting in constant worry and anxiety despite being materially well-off.

The color of the crown chakra is white or purple. Crystals that heal this chakra are clear quartz, amethyst, charoite, howlite, and selenite.

Therefore, when you walk into a crystal store or shop online for them, you can choose your crystal based on which chakra you want to be healed. Picking the right crystal is a combination of your intuitive powers and knowledge that you gain.

# Chapter Two: Important and Popular Crystals and Their Healing Properties

The world of crystals and gemstones is so large that it can overwhelm a beginner. There are a mind-boggling number of crystals available on the market so that deciding what you want can be quite intimidating. This chapter is dedicated to giving you some basic insights into some of the crystals that are both popular and important for healing.

The first 7-10 crystals are must-haves. The others that follow can be looked at once you delve deeper into this amazing and magical world and discover for yourself what you really want. Let's dive right in.

## Clear Quartz – The Master Healer

This crystal is a great first choice for a beginner. It is the most iconic representative of the quartz family of crystals and is abundantly available everywhere on Earth because it can develop in any kind of environmental circumstance. Having been on this planet for so many eons, clear quartz has found its way into nearly tribe and community's folklore.

Quartz has its etymological roots in the Greek word for 'ice.' The ancient Greek philosophers and wise men like Theophrastus and others believed that this beautiful transparent stone was some form of permanent ice. They believed that water had solidified so deeply that it could not revert back to its liquid state, and this kind of 'permanently solidified water' was called quartz.

Clear quartz is called the master healer because of its amazing versatility and its ability to smoothen out energy flows in all the chakras. It can be programmed for any purpose. Clear quartz cannot only direct its own energy for effective healing but can also enhance the healing power of other crystals. It brings clarity to your thoughts and enhances the strength and brightness of your aura.

Different cultures had different reasons for using clear quartz for healing. The Japanese believed that clear quartz was the 'perfect jewel' because it represented space, patience and purity. Tribal cultures in North American offered clear quartz as food along with other offerings to their gods.

Some of the South American and Australian cultures have woven their origin or creational stories around clear quartz. They believed that creator life is a cosmic serpent that was coiled and held in clear quartz. In some other South American and Central American cultures, clear quartz was sacred because they believed that, like an urn, it held the spirits of their ancestors. These people believed that the metaphysical properties of clear quartz could heal the illnesses of their cattle.

Clear quartz is an essential crystal needed during crystal-based healing for its programmability and amplification properties. Although this crystal is not connected to any one particular Zodiac sign, it is believed to have the power to temper down the power desires of the Leos and the adamant nature of the Capricorns.

## Tiger's Eye – The Stone for Confidence

The tiger's eye is a perfect start to build self-esteem and confidence. This beautiful golden brown tiger-stripped stone is replete with a masculine kind of energy. It is the ultimate power crystal and can help you free yourself from self-doubt created either by your own past failures or by jealous people in your life. It is also excellent for grounding purposes.

This gemstone is also referred to as chatoyancy, which is French for cat, and if including in your daily meditation can fuel your deepest passions. The tiger's eye resonates with the solar plexus chakra and is connected with making money. It teaches you the most essential aspect of economics, which is 'with increased productivity comes increased wealth and money.'

The tiger's eye stone empowers you with the motivation needed to make things happen and realize your dreams and desires. Moreover, this crystal helps you balance your power by living a life of honesty and integrity to achieve success. After all, the tiger is the largest cat in the world, and yet it allows the lion to be the king of the jungle.

The tiger's eye can be your personal life coach who gives you the strength and motivation to come out of your dream world and work hard to make those dreams come true. It empowers you with risk-taking capabilities and drives you to move out of your comfort zone; both key elements for success, expansion, and growth.

## Amethyst – The Psychic Powerhouse

Although suitable for most novices in the crystal world, it is important to keep in mind that this beautiful violet crystal with a name as lilting as amethyst has great powers to develop and expand your psychic capabilities.

It is found abundantly in Bolivia, Brazil, Africa, Mexico, Canada, and other parts of Europe and the US. Despite its wide prevalence, amethyst is one of the most revered crystals since time immemorial. The ancient Romans and Greeks associated amethyst with luxury and, therefore, the highly regarded stone was found in royal rings, crowns and scepters.

Catholic clergymen wore amethyst because they believed it had the powers to inspire celibacy and piety. The ancient Greeks believed that the power to inhibit intoxication was bestowed on this crystal by Bacchus, the Greek God of wine, fertility, and agriculture, and therefore, this stone was worn to prevent hangovers and drunkenness. The Chinese Feng Shui philosophers associated amethyst with wealth, and if placed in the wealth corner of the house, can bring in prosperity.

Amethyst is connected with the crown chakra and is believed to help you connect with your deepest spiritual powers, and if you are not prepared to handle this situation, then it could unnerve you a bit. And yet, amethyst is the perfect beginner's choice for protection and to cleanse your body and surroundings of all kinds of negative energies.

Amethyst can help clear negative energies resulting from anxiety and stress. It helps in purification of the mind and building your spiritual and psychic powers. Many people meditate with an amethyst held in their palms to rid themselves of confusion and darkness.

Amethyst is an effective healer for work-related anxieties and stress and for stress associated with the lack of money, wealth and abundance. Your communication and intuitive powers can also be enhanced with the healing power of the amethyst crystal. Keeping an amethyst in your office space will help you include your intuitive powers with intellect and knowledge to take tough but effective decisions for improved business success. An amethyst placed in the family room will increase familial bonding and frees up the atmosphere for open and honest conversations among loved ones.

## Hematite – The Bouncer Crystal

This powerful deflector of negative energies protects you from psychic attacks. It deflects negative energy aimed at you and transfers it to Mother Earth for healing. Therefore, it is called as the Bouncer Crystal. If for any inexplicable reason you feel drawn to hematite, then it is quite likely that you are in search of grounding and stability.

The minute you touch a hematite crystal, you will feel centered and calm. It is the perfect crystal to cleanse and clear the root chakra, and subsequently, achieve the calming effects of grounding yourself. Hematite offers an immense sense of stability.

The hematite crystal absorbs all the toxic emotions and energies that are holding you back from achieving your potential. It clears all negative energies connected to stress, worry and anxiety. By grounding you to Mother Earth and increasing the power of your root chakra, hematite enhances self-confidence and power during stressful times.

In addition to healing your mental worries and stresses, hematite is known to cleanse and clear your circulatory system. Found in abundance in Australia, hematite got its name because of the red color rendered by the high content of iron in this stone. "Haima' is the Latin word for blood, and that explains the etymology of hematite. Hematite is perfect to calm your troubled mind by simply grounding you and strengthening your root chakra.

**Rose Quartz – The Mother of all Crystals**

Gentle, soothing and calming properties characterize the rose quartz crystal. It is a great healer of emotional pain. It opens and clears the energy blockages in the heart chakra enhancing your capability of loving everyone including yourself. Connected to the heart chakra, this is the perfect self-love stone for beginners.

A gemstone for the hopeless romantic from time immemorial rose quartz has been a permanent fixture in love rituals for centuries. Like the clear quartz, this is also a member of the quartz family and is primarily made of silicon dioxide. The soft, pink color is a result of irradiation as well as the minute inclusions of pink-colored fibers within the stone.

The irradiation effect is why it is essential to keep rose quartz out in the sun to prevent it from losing its natural pink color. The rose quartz is found in plenty all over the world, and largely in Madagascar, Brazil, South Africa, and India. The early Egyptian, Roman and Greek civilizations used rose quartz talismans to represent a negotiated deal.

The symbol of love was first attached to this beautiful pink stone by Roman and Greek myths. It is believed that the blood of Aphrodite and her lover Adonis is what gives this crystal a pink color. Another legend says that Eros, the Greek God of love gave the rose quartz to human beings as a symbol of love.

While the romantic kind of love is what is popularly connected with the rose quartz crystal, in reality, this crystal represents unconditional love. The rose quartz can take your consciousness to a higher level thereby empowering you to accept and give love unconditionally. It helps you look at conflicts and fights in different perspectives, which, in turn, helps you, forgive and move on in the relationship.

Additionally, rose quartz awakens the spirit of self-love and self-compassion and empowers you to forgive yourself too. This magical gemstone cleans toxins in the form of negative emotions and energies from your body and mind. Hold rose quartz close to your heart to begin the unbridled and unconditional journey of love.

## Turquoise – Another Master Healer

Believed to be the spiritual energy bridge between human beings and the divine, turquoise is another master healer among crystals. Since ancient times, turquoise has been worn for its ability to bring good luck to and protect the wearer. It was worn by the likes of King Tutankhamen and Queen Cleopatra for its amazing protective ability.

Moreover, if you give or receive this beautiful blue-green crystal as a gift, then its healing powers increase multifold. Turquoise is also effective to improve communication as it helps you speak the truth always, irrespective of the repercussions. Turquoise symbolizes the oceans of the world.

The warriors in the ancient times wore an amulet embedded with turquoise before starting off on any battle for the crystal's personal protection capabilities. The Aztecs too wore this crystal on battle gear and ceremonial masks. Persian legends hold that when turquoise reflects the moonlight, then it is supposed to bring good luck.

Today, turquoise is used to heal wounded hearts and to smooth out chronic forms of stress. This crystal promotes energetic flow empowered by the highest energy frequency namely love. Additionally, like quartz, turquoise is highly versatile and can be programmed for specific healing intentions.

You can program your turquoise crystal as a good luck charm, to realign and balance your chakras, or clear the spiritual path to reach higher levels of consciousness. Hold it in your hand as you perform your daily meditation, and feel uplifted by its calming and soothing effect brought on by the world's most beloved emotional food; love.

## Citrine – The Prosperity Crystal and the Light Maker

This orange-hued crystal is known for its ability to attract wealth and prosperity into your life. Closely connected to the solar plexus chakra, it is also known to boost self-confidence and self-worth. Citrine can clear any aura of negativities resulting in an increased intensity of positivity.

Citrine oozes light energy and emanates joy and positivity. Citrine gets its name from the French word for lemon and is undoubtedly connected to the sun and the joy it is capable of spreading. It is found abundantly and in its natural state in Spain, Brazil, Russia, Africa, Madagascar, the US, and other countries too.

Citrine has been used to increase the aura and beauty of ornaments since ancient times. It found its way into Scottish men's wear in the form of shoulder poaches, kilt pins, and to brighten swords and daggers, thanks to Queen Victoria's affinity for this yellow-hued beautiful crystal.

Citrine's healing powers lie in its capabilities to clear energy blockages in the sacral, solar plexus, and the third chakras to boost your creativity and spiritual progress. It increases your sexual and fertility energies as well. Citrine placed in the bedroom can increase intimacy, and when placed in the office space can bring in prosperity and success. In children's rooms, citrine brings in a sense of security through the golden light of the sun.

Citrine being the crystal of happiness and sunlight holds no negativity and is almost purely positive. It reminds you to live in the present moment instead of worrying about your past or future.

## Bloodstone – The Energy Crystal

Bloodstone represents vitality, courage, strength, and purification.

Known for its ability to overcome lethargy, this energy-inducing crystal purifies blood too. It helps to overcome negative thoughts and feelings and is a great energy booster. Additionally, the uplifting and purifying bloodstone crystal increases drive and motivation and boosts enthusiasm too.

During the Middle Ages, the red spots in the red-green stone were believed to be the blood of Christ, which seemed to render the crystal with magical powers. The green color of the crystal was thought to represent the power of the Earth, and the wearer of bloodstone is protected from negative effects and negative energy.

Summarily, bloodstone works to stabilize and ground your physical and mental powers while increasing your courage, strength, and determination to take on and overcome challenges that obstruct your pathway to success.

## Carnelian – The Creativity and Action Crystal

Carnelian has the power to remove energy blocks in your mind that are preventing your creativity reaching its potential. Such negative energies dominate your mind and you feel burned out and completely uninspired. The powerful orange hue of the carnelian crystal sparks your passion and drives you to move ahead. It is an action that motivates and compels you to find joy and happiness by pushing you to realize your dreams and desires.

In the ancient times, carnelian was found on breastplate armor because of its ability to render courage and strength to the warrior who carried it. Whenever you feel stifled by stage fright, hold a carnelian in your hand, and watch the fear dissolve into nothingness.

The early Egyptians always wore carnelian on their bodies because they believed in its power to restore and renew strength and vitality. Today, carnelian stone is prescribed for increasing personal power, creativity and courage. Carnelian also diminishes the power of negative emotions such as jealousy, fear, anger, and resentment so that you are more in control of your life. With the power of carnelian on your side, you feel calm, healthy, strong, and happy.

## Celestite – The Stress-Relieving Crystal

The Latin word for celestial (or heavenly) is 'caelestis' which is the root of the name of the celestite crystal. The divine blue color of celestite inspires calmness and tranquility. You simply need to gaze at this beautiful hue to feel balanced and peaceful.

When you place this crystal on any part of your body, the tension in that area will be released, and your muscles will feel relaxed. When placed in your bedroom, celestite can help you get a restful sleep. The celestite crystal is perfect for the chaotic mind. The feelings associated with this crystal are serenity, calmness, uplifting, and soothing.

If you are an impulsive person, then celestite is the perfect crystal to cool you down. Taking rash decisions or behaving rashly in the heat of the moment can only worsen the situation. If you feel your temper is getting in the way of the clarity of your thoughts, then celestite is the crystal to reach out to.

## Selenite – The Liquid Light

This gorgeous looking crystal is sometimes referred to as Satin Spar for the milky sheen that radiates from its surface. Selenite is used extensively by metaphysical healers to improve well-being and for protection. It is found abundantly across the globe including the USA, Mexico, Australia, and Greece. However, most healers prefer the Mexican selenite for effective healing work.

Selenite is a very soft stone, and therefore, quite flexible. It gets its name from the Greek Moon Goddess, Selene, for this reason; when the crystal reflects moonlight, it looks like a drop of the moon has landed on the Earth. Although selenite is very soft, its metaphysical healing powers are phenomenal. Its most useful property is the rock's ability to help you activate your higher levels of consciousness by aligning all your chakras.

Selenite has the power to compel honesty and integrity in people who are under its aura. It clears energy blockages and allows the vibrations to flow through your body and mind as smoothly as a liquid. Healers use selenite to connect with guardian angels and spirit guides. These crystals can also multiply the effects of other crystals when they are used in tandem. Using selenite in the crystal grid (more about crystal grids in Chapter Four) in your home can help to keep out toxic influences.

## Tourmaline – The Energy Cleanser

Tourmaline is an excellent cleanser of energy fields. It facilitates the removal of negative thought patterns and other forms of negative energies. It acts like a bodyguard saving you from the world's negativities. Known for its powerful capability to absorb electromagnetic radiation, tourmaline is perfect to keep near computers and other electronic devices to keep your body and mind safe from the harmful effects of radiations.

Simply place a tumbled stone of tourmaline in a bowl of water in your main living area, and you will feel a noticeable reduction in negativities and prickly thought patterns that were hitherto thwarting your progress. Its natural black color allows this energy-absorbing crystal to consume all wavelengths of all colors. Tourmaline is great to use when you are overcome by phobias and fears as it will simply ingest your anxieties like a sponge.

When you wear tourmaline on your body like in a piece of jewelry or accessory, it is like wearing a sign that tells the negative powers of the universe that they cannot cross the line. Carrying it in your pocket will ensure you don't pick up other people's negative aura. Connected with the root chakra, tourmaline helps you feel secure and grounded.

## Onyx – The Crystal for Letting Go

The onyx is known for its amazing ability to root out fear from your system. Fear is one of the most toxic and debilitating emotions, and when you let go of fear, there is nothing to stop you from reaching your fullest potential. When you let go of fears, you find the courage to fall into the deepest depths of your soul helping you find things that otherwise remain completely hidden.

The onyx crystal has three bands of colors including white, gray, and black. White is the color of the day sky, black is the color of the night sky, and gray is the color of the dusk and pre-dawn skies. The powers of healing and magic are most intense during the dusk and pre-dawn times when change is taking place at the optimal intensity. These three colors of the onyx crystal represent the interconnectedness of the black-and-white of the world.

Onyx is highly effective to heal anxieties and worries as it soothes and calms the frazzled and frenetic thoughts of your mind. You can use it to heal cracks that keep appearing in your work-life balance. And when you feel fear, reach out for that onyx in your crystal box. Hold it to your heart, and send a wish to the universe to be relieved of this debilitating fear. And watch your fears dissolve into nothingness.

## Calcite – The Energy Amplifier

Two of the most commonly used calcite stones are green and orange, although this gemstone is available in a huge variety of colors and types. The combination of these two calcite crystals has the power to magnify and amplify the energy of the other crystals used in the healing process. Calcite comes from the Greek word for 'lime.'

Green calcite, by itself, is excellent for attracting prosperity and good fortune. In addition, the color green helps you connect with the natural world. When you meditate with a green calcite in your hand, you will discover ways to draw energy from Earth's life source. Moreover, the soothing green color will keep reminding you of the immense power latent in nature and will teach you to be grateful for this beautiful life in the midst of magical nature.

## Jade – The Lucky Charm Crystal

Jade is deeply connected with the heart chakra. It is the ultimate good luck charm, and its powerful vibrational energy brings in abundance and prosperity into your life. Jade was one of the most sought-after gemstones in the Chinese civilization, and this tradition continues even to this day. Jade stones were used on the crowns and tombstones of Chinese emperors.

The green color of the jade crystal reflects the pristine and beautiful vegetation of Mother Earth. In the same way as green plants can provide food for the entire world by harnessing the power of sunlight, the jade crystal can harness the metaphysical powers of the sunlight for your well-being, growth, and vitality.

Jade is also the crystal of eternal youth and is used extensively in facial and skin treatments. People use jade rollers over their faces to allow the natural rejuvenating power of jade to smoothen out wrinkles and restore the youthfulness of their facial skin.

Meditate with a jade crystal in your hand, and leverage the power of good fortune as it enters your life. Jade crystal also helps you feel gratitude for all the good things in your life.

## Amazonite – The Optimism Crystal

Reflecting the verdant foliage of the beautiful, lush Amazonian region, amazonite is also a great stone to draw good luck to your life. Amazonite is referred to as the anti-anxiety medication in the world of crystals. Amazonite is called as the 'hope stone,' as it helps to fill your heart and mind with a can-do attitude.

It has the power to clear away and cleanse all the negative psychic debris accumulated in your system. Hold it close to your heart, and watch all the toxic emotions leaving your body and mind leaving you stress-free and filled with optimism for the future.

The crystals mentioned in this chapter offer you only a glimpse into the wonderful and powerful world of crystals and gemstones. First, experiment with these crystals, and as your intuitive power and knowledge of the world of universal vibrational energy progresses, you can delve deeper.

# Chapter Three: Taking Care of Crystals

Once you received a crystal, you become its guardian. It is your duty to purify its energies and keep it from getting corrupted and unusable. The reason for having to take care of crystals is because they have the power to absorb all kinds of energies around them including the negative ones. Therefore, cleansing, charging, programming, and other aspects need to be done so that your crystals are clean, clear and add value to your life.

There are primarily two parts to taking care of crystals and they are:

- Cleansing
- Recharging
- Programming

## Cleansing Your Crystals

As mentioned earlier, crystals absorb energies from their surroundings. Cleansing them will facilitate the removal of negative energies so that they are ready to be charged and programmed for any specific purpose. The first time you need to cleanse your crystal is as soon as you get it for the first time, irrespective of whether it was gifted to you or you purchased it yourself.

After that, you must cleanse your crystal regularly depending on how often you use it and for what purpose. The crystals you wear or have around in your house need to be cleansed more regularly than those you use only occasionally for healing purpose. The crystals used on a daily basis are interacting with other surrounding energies at varying frequencies. Moreover, you will also know when your crystal needs cleansing. For example:

- Most crystals will lose their luster if you have not cleansed them.
- Quartz crystal will become cloudy instead of clear and bright which is its natural profile.
- Some crystals will be heavier and denser than before; it will seem that they are carrying an extra burden, which is nothing but the negative energies that they have absorbed.
- If you are wearing it on your body, then you will notice that it is not emitting the same vibrational energy that it was giving out before.
- If you have used your crystal(s) for a particularly intense energy situation such as an illness or a trauma, then cleansing of your crystal(s) after the session becomes important.
- You will also need to cleanse your crystal before reprogramming it for a different purpose.

***Methods of Cleansing*** – There are different ways of cleansing your crystals. Some of them are described below. Try all of them, and identify which one works best for a particular gemstone as each crystal calls for a different cleansing method for optimum efficiency. Also, cleansing methods are person-specific, and therefore, try many methods, and choose what works for you and your crystal(s) the best.

Before you start off, it is important that you clear your own mind, and create a strong intention for the cleansing process. Crystals hold vibrational energies that are bound to get altered and affected by the impurities and other forms of discords they experience during their entire life cycle. Therefore, cleansing crystals calls for a strong intention to ensure they achieve a clear and pure state.

Here is a small ritual to get the right intention before the cleansing process. Hold the crystal(s) in your hand, and imagine them immersed in a white light. Visualize all the unwanted energies being spirited away into oblivion. Imagine your crystal(s) in a re-energized, natural, and pure state. Ask the universe to help restore your gemstones to their original and full energy potential.

Remain in this position for a little while or until you feel satisfied with your efforts at getting the right intention. And finally, pray and ask all the energies in the universe to facilitate the transformation of your crystal(s) into divine love and light.

After your mind is clear with the cleansing intention, clear the room using sage, bells, or even a simple mantra. This clearing refers to clearing negative energies. Of course, ensure the cleansing space is clear of physical clutter as well. The cleansing process is a ritual, and for any ritual to achieve success, you need to have a calm, peaceful, and serene atmosphere both mentally and physically.

*Cleansing with flowing water* – Water is a universal healer, and crystals and water have a long and old legacy. They work very well with each other, and therefore, using water to cleanse your crystal is one of the easiest and most effective methods. Here is what you can do:

- Hold the crystal under water. Although a river, ocean, rainwater, or natural spring is preferred, in a modern urban setting, this may not be possible. So, you can hold your gemstones under running tap water.
- Imagine the pure water removing all the negativities trapped inside the crystal. Imagine the energy and frequency disruptions within the

crystal structure being smoothened out, and the negativities dissolving in the water and being eliminated.

- Use a little sea salt to rub over the crystal, and again place it under water for the salt to be cleansed away too.
- Let your gemstones dry out naturally under sunlight.

An important word of caution; some crystals cannot withstand being cleansed in water. For example, selenite will simply dissolve. Therefore, research your crystal and choose your method wisely. Also, remember to use cold running water. Do not use warm or hot water for cleansing purposes.

*Cleansing with salt water* – Some types (not all) are cleansed thoroughly with salt water. You can either choose to use sea water or plain water mixed with sea salt. If you cannot get sea salt, then normal cooking salt is fine too. Fill a glass bowl with water, dissolve some salt, and let your crystals lie fully submerged inside for 1-24 hours depending on the crystal, and the duration of the elapsed time since the last time you cleansed it.

After you remove the crystal from the salt water, ensure you thoroughly clean it in cool, refreshing running water to completely remove all traces of salt. The salt water used to cleanse the crystal should be discarded as it will have absorbed all the accumulated unwanted and negative energies from the crystals.

***Cleansing with moonlight*** – The moon's energy frequencies are empowered for purification. The moonlight's cleansing capabilities have been harnessed by crystal healers from time immemorial. The moon radiates feminine energy, which can help in emotional and spiritual healing as well. Simply place your crystals under the moonlight either on a full moon or new moon day, and allow them to harness the moon's powerful energy frequencies.

***Cleansing with sunlight*** – The power of the sun and its radiating light is as powerful as the moon. It would be naïve not to harness this amazing energy of the star of our solar system. Unlike the moon, the sun's energy frequencies are more masculine than feminine.

Place your crystals under the direct sunlight and allow the power of the radiant light to smoothen our energy wrinkles within the stones and eliminate all negativities from within.

***Cleansing with snow*** – For those unfortunate enough to have access to blessed, beautiful snow, it can be an amazing crystal cleanser. Putting your crystals in snow is a fast and powerful method to cleanse and clear them of all negative and burdening energies.

***Cleansing with earth*** – When you bury your crystals in the warmth of Mother Earth, you are effectively sending them back to their home. And nothing can soothe and cleanse more than a mother's love. All forms of lingering negativities will be cleared out of your favorite crystals. You can bury your crystals for 3, 7 or 11 days for the best cleansing effect. The power of your crystals will be completely reset and rejuvenated.

***Cleansing with smoke*** – Smudging is a cleansing process where you use the smoke of sage, lavender, cedar, sweetgrass, copal, or other naturally-empowered sacred herbs to cleanse the surroundings. Smudging is also an effective cleansing method for crystals.

First, light the herbs and let them burn. After the flames die down, smoke will be created from the embers. Pass your crystals through this smoke while visualizing the negative energies being cleared away from them. Using smoke for cleansing is especially good for crystals embedded in jewelry. Such items could potentially corrode if you tried using water.

***Cleansing with rock salt*** – Place your gemstones in a bed of salt for about 1-2 days. This helps in the purification of the crystal's energy matrix.

***Cleansing with sound*** – The power of certain sound frequencies has the power to cleanse and charge. The tinkle of a bell is one such sound energy. Just tinkle a bell close to your crystal(s), and visualize your gemstones being cleared of all negativities. Similarly, the sound of your voice and other sacred chants are used for charging and programming.

***Cleansing with other crystals*** – A few crystals actually do not need any cleansing or clearing. Moreover, their energy frequencies are so unique that these crystals can help to clear and cleanse other crystals. Such rare treasures in the crystal world include carnelian, selenite, kyanite, amethyst, etc.

Place all your crystals under a slab of selenite, and you can rest assured that they will be cleared and cleansed of all negative energies. You can also use a cluster of amethyst in this way.

## Recharging Your Crystals

Recharging of crystals typically happens when you cleanse them because the elements for cleansing also help to recharge your crystal's energy frequencies.

However, you can cleanse and recharge separately too. After you finish cleansing your gemstones, create a new intention to recharge them with renewed energy.

Hold your crystals in your hand, and visualize a beam of a bright, white light entering them, and renewing the power of the crystal matrix. Hold this picture until you are satisfied with the strength of your intention, and begin your recharging process. Here is a quick summary to help you:

- Place your crystals under the bright and beautiful light of the sun. A sunbath renders an amazing glow to your crystals as their energy levels are restored to their full potential. Placing the crystals on the earth to receive sunlight will enhance the recharging process.
- Place your gemstones under the powerful moonlight on a full moon. Renewed energy will penetrate the crystals by the effect of the gentle moonlight.
- You can place your crystals in dynamic weather conditions such as a thunderstorm. This method will empower your gemstone with an amazing electromagnetic charge.
- An amethyst cluster is a great crystal charger, especially those that are etched in jewelry and small-sized crystals for which other charging methods mentioned above may not be suitable.

Your gemstones are work best and their energies remain ever fresh when they out in the open. Avoid using artificial materials to place your crystals in your office or your home. Use natural materials such as silk or velvet. Additionally, your crystals are fragile and can chip or break. Therefore, it is essential that you handle them with care. Carry your crystals in velvet, cotton, satin, or silk holders or bags.

## Precautions to be Taken While Storing Your Crystals

Always store your gemstones in a clean and dry place. Exposure to moisture and dust can damage certain types of crystals. Also, if you live in a coastal area, then your crystals need to be protected against excessive exposure to salt air.

There could be some gemstones, which you would have bought with a lot of love, and you may have spent a lot of money too. For such pieces, it would be best if you stored them in boxes made of good-quality plastic or any other acid-free and inert materials to prevent any kind of chemical reactions between the crystal and the container.

For small pieces of crystals, buy yourself a good-sized box with multiple compartments, preferably lined with velvet or silk. Each crystal can be kept in one little compartment. This will look good and each gemstone will be nicely protected too. Keeping all together in one bunch can result in the harder and bigger crystals chipping and damaging the smaller and softer ones.

Also, avoid using cotton pads or balls as some kind of cushion because the fibers can stick to the corners of your special gemstones resulting in disrupting the energy frequencies. Tumbled stones or other polished items can be kept anywhere without much fuss.

Remember every specimen of crystal you have is unique. It is mined at specific geographic locations and has a unique geologic and genetic background. Once damaged and lost, you can never really replace the identical crystal with the exact same set of energy frequency. Crystals are divine treasures gifted to us by nature and Mother Earth, and therefore taking care of them is our duty and responsibility.

## Programming Crystals

Programming a crystal is a ritual in which you assign special powers to your crystal to help you achieve a specific task or job. You could program your crystal to help you with your work, to help you in your relationships, to attract prosperity and abundance, to attract love, etc. You could program one crystal for each of these intentions and place them in strategic locations either at home or in your workplace.

Another useful program to input into a crystal is to help you to recall your dreams at night. Many times, the universe sends out powerful signs through dreams. And sadly, we don't make enough effort to try and recall our dreams except for the ones that really scare us. Program a crystal with this particular task, and keep it under your pillow. In the morning, hold the crystal in your palm as you try to recall your dreams as vividly as you can.

So, how do you program a gemstone? Here are a few helpful steps you can follow:

- First, decide what help you seek from the crystal.
- Choose a crystal that you are drawn to for this task, and ask if the gemstone is willing to partner with you in your endeavor. If the crystal's intentions are not aligned with yours, then you will get a definite sign of resistance for a 'No' answer. And, it is quite easy to discern the negative answer from a crystal. Positive answers, on the other hand, are tricky to determine. Many times, it is a neutral feeling you get when you put forward the willingness question to the crystal.
- Once you have chosen the right crystal, hold it first to your heart chakra, and then to your third eye chakra. Now, with a clear mind and intent, visualize your task or project being projected into

the crystal. Extend this imagination outward until you see your heart, eye, and mind forming a triangle and locking your intent.
- Lastly, state your purpose aloud for the energies of the universe to hear.
- Give thanks to the crystal for its willingness to transmit your desire through its energy frequency

As you delve deeper into the realm of crystals, you will discover your own special powers of connecting with the energy frequency of crystals, and use the resultant resonating power for your own good and for that of others. Crystals are a boon to us, and we have to treat them with the utmost respect.

# Chapter Four: Placement of Crystals for Everyday Benefits

In the world of crystals, everything and everyone is connected to each other and one another. Everything in the universe is nothing but a form of vibrational energy. The energies of different things and different people work at different frequencies, and when these frequencies resonate, then the result is optimum harmony, joy, and happiness.

Crystals have the power to work their magic and bring together the connecting frequencies to create harmony and health, and consequently, positive change. And that is the reason why crystals are powerful tools to heal, harmonize and eliminate negative energies within and outside of you. Here are some practical ways you can use crystals easily for effective healing and happiness.

1. ***Keep a crystal in your proximity right through the day***

Determine what kind of healing you want. What kind of frequency shift are you seeking in your vibrational energy? Based on these answers, choose the appropriate crystal. Cleanse it using one of the methods discussed in Chapter Three. Then, program the crystal for your specific purpose by creating the right intent using the following steps:

- Hold the crystal in your hand.
- Next, think of the problems for which you are seeking help from the crystals. Bring forth all the feelings and thoughts connected with your desired outcome.
- Imagine the outcome has already taken place, and you are enjoying its benefits.
- Transfer these positive thoughts into the crystal and imagine a white light passing through it and locking your purpose within the gemstone.
- Thank the crystal for helping you.
- The crystal's vibrational energy is now programmed to align with yours.

Now, keep this programmed crystal in your pocket or around your neck. Keep it on your body until you feel and believe that the gemstone's vibrational energy field has entered your own aura, and the combined energy fields are resonating effects are helping to bring about positive changes. Remember to cleanse and reprogram this crystal regularly to refresh, renew, and recharge its vibrational energy.

## 2. *Keep a crystal under your pillow every night*

Crystals with vibrational energies suited for relaxation and restfulness are perfect to be placed under your pillow each night. For example, black tourmaline is a great gemstone that helps to remove all the harsh, frenetic and negative vibes and energies you might have absorbed during the day.

These negativities could be in any form ranging from the excessive exposure to harmful electromagnetic waves of electronic devices to the negative aura of people you would have interacted with throughout the day. Other gemstones are helpful in healing the physical and mental wounds received during the day include spirit quartz, selenite, Jasper, and amethyst.

Amethyst is also helpful if you have problems recalling your dreams. Remember the universe employs dreams to send you signs, and it would be unfortunate if you could not recall your dreams. Other crystals that can help in this include dream quartz (a greenish-pink colored gemstone that is difficult to find and expensive too) and hemimorphite (a beautiful blue stone that reminds you of a gorgeous icy glacier).

### 3. *Place crystals in strategic places in your home and office*

For example, if you want an organized and clutter-free vibe in your workspace, then fluorite is a great crystal to have on your desk. A white quartz crystal is great for all kinds of spaces and areas. It helps in uplifting, positive vibrations and cleansing the environment.

Tiger's eye or aventurine attracts wealth and prosperity. So, place one or both in your living room or business space. Orange crystals like carnelian, citrine, sodalite, and others imbue intimacy in the surroundings and are excellent for placing in bedrooms.

In addition to healing and cleansing benefits, crystals are great for adding some oomph and oeuvre to your décor. Their beauty and shine can enhance the aesthetics of any room.

### 4. *Place a suitable crystal over your goal and dream lists*

First, create a dream list in the present tense and not in the future tense. For example, don't write, "I want to be healthy and strong." Write, "I am healthy, strong, and full of vitality." Suppose this is your top desire because you have been plagued by various physical illnesses in the recent past.

Take a crystal whose vibrational energy is in sync with your goal. For example, green aventurine or onyx are excellent for building energy and vitality. So, fold the paper on which you have written down your intentions for strength and vitality, and place the chosen crystal over it. You can place it on the altar (if you have one). If you don't have an altar, you can place it anywhere where it will not be disturbed.

The crystal behaves like a battery and charges up your intention, and direct the universal energy to manifest your outcomes.

5. *Use crystals to cleanse and clear up your personal energy and/or aura*

If your physical space is dusty and unclean, don't you use a brush to clear up the area, and make it clean again? Some crystals work just like brushes or brooms to cleanse and clear up negativities trapped in the field of your personal aura.

For example, a selenite wand can identify, and pull out negative energy patterns from the energy field of your personal aura to neutralize and dissolve them into nothingness. Wave the selenite wand all over your body in a brushing action. Keep the wand about a foot away from your body while doing this cleansing action.

Another effective way of cleansing your personal aura is to direct all frenetic and harsh energies to black crystals such as obsidian, smoky quartz, or tourmaline. Hold one such crystal in your hand, and consciously transfer all the negativities to the crystal. When you have done this, place the crystal in bright sunlight to allow the trapped negativities to evaporate into the atmosphere.

## 6. *Put crystal essences into your drinking water*

Crystal essences or gem elixirs are a convenient way to harness the benefits of the vibrational energies of crystals. They can be made easily and stored for later use. Moreover, these crystal essences are also found in stores.

You can use one, two, or more crystals to make your gem elixir. A combination of crystals results in an advantageous blend of all the synergies of the gemstones used. The total synergy of vibrations of many crystals is invariably more than the sum of all of them. The following steps help you to prepare the gem elixir at home:

***Required items*** - Get the following items ready before you start the preparation process.

- Choose the crystal(s) you want to make the elixir of. You can include similar types of crystals (for examples, different types of quartzes) to enhance the charge of the essence.
- Two containers made of glass or any other food-safe materials; the sizes should be such that one should fit into the other with a little gap available between the two. For example, you can take a glass jar that fits into a glass bowl with some room available between the two.
- Two dark-colored bottles of different sizes
- A glass stopper
- Distilled water or spring water
- Any variety of vinegar or vodka (80 proof or higher) – this is the preservative
- A calm and steady mind with a clear intention to create a powerful gem elixir

***How to make crystal essence*** - You can make this potion outdoors or indoors as long as you get sufficient sunlight or moonlight for the process. You can also use your personal space or altar (if you have one) to prepare the elixir.

- First, clear, cleanse, and charge the crystals.
- Next, center yourself, and create the right intention with prayers and breathing techniques.

- Say your intention aloud so that the divine energies and the crystals prepare themselves to help you in your endeavor.
- Place the large container in the determined space.
- Place the small container inside the large container. Ensure the position is stable, and that it will not topple over.
- Fill as much of water as you can into the larger container ensuring that nothing falls into the small container.
- Arrange the crystals in the small container.
- State your intent again, and the crystals and water in the designated place for at least four hours.
- Then, gently pour out the crystal-charged water from the large container into the larger of the two bottles. Pour the water until it is halfway full.
- Pour vodka or vinegar until the bottle is full. This preservative helps to 'fix' the vibrational energy of the crystals in the water.
- Transfer a small amount of this elixir into the smaller of the two bottles for immediate use. You can use distilled water or spring water to dilute this elixir if you want.
- Thank the crystal(s) and the divine energies for helping you create the gem elixir.

Store the larger bottle of this amazing gem elixir safely for future use. You can refrigerate the crystal essence for a few days. But, you must use it quickly. Alternately, you can make crystal essence in the same way in smaller quantities for immediate use in which case you do not need to add any preservatives. It is important not to put crystals directly into the water as the soft ones will dissolve.

If you don't want to go through the rigmarole of making your own elixir, you can use store-bought ones too. Add a few drops into your drinking water and you are, in effect, bringing the crystals' vibration into your own vibrational energy, which can result in powerful changes for you.

7. *Create crystal grids*

If you have multiple crystals, then you can make a crystal grid to create positive changes in your life. Making the effort to create the grid itself can result in positive changes. However, you can get added benefits if you let loose your creativity, and make a crystal that resonates with the vibrational powers of all the crystals involved in the grid. Additionally, the Universal Divine energy will also open doors for you.

You can use a geometric pattern of your choice, though the 'mandala' is one of the most powerful and popular grid pattern used by experts in the crystal world. The geometric pattern also adds its own to the potent mix of crystal energies. In fact, if made correctly and creatively, the energy of a crystal grid is almost palpable.

***How to create a crystal grid*** – Use the following steps to create your own crystal grid in your home:

- A suitable undisturbed space in your home.
- A small piece of paper in which you have written your intent.
- A central crystal; typically, this central piece would be a crystal point that would help in transmitting your intention out into the universe. However, any good crystal will also work.
- Tumbled stone crystals whose vibrational energies are aligned with your purpose.
- A crystal grid garment or cloth; this is optional though it enhances the power of the grid.

First, determine your intention for the crystal grid. What do you want?

- Do you want to attract prosperity, wealth, and abundance?
- Do you want health and fitness?
- Do you want peace of mind?
- Do you want improved creativity?
- Do you want to attract love?

The more specific your intentions are, the easier it is to choose the right crystals for the grid. You can create a crystal grid for any intention of your choice. There are no restrictions at all.

- Next, choose the crystals that are aligned with your intentions. For example, for prosperity and abundance, you will need gold and green crystals such as citrine, aventurine, pyrite, etc. For health, you will need purple and blue gemstones like Angelite, sodalite, fluorite, etc. There are no right or wrong answers for the type of crystals you use for your crystal grid. Choose the gemstones that you feel drawn to, and feel intuitively positive.
- Cleanse and recharge your crystals. Cleanse the crystal grid space too.
- Spread your crystal grid cloth, and in its center, place a piece of paper with your intentions written down.
- Next, state your intention aloud.
- Start placing the crystals in the grid beginning from the outward boundary moving towards the center. As you put each crystal in its place, ensure you are visualizing or thinking about your intentions.
- Lastly, place the central crystal on top of the written intention.
- Now, activate the crystal grid. For this, take a crystal point, and draw an invisible line running through all the crystals on the grid. Think of the 'connecting the dots' game you used to play as a child.

With this, your crystal grid is activated, and its energy will begin to do its magic in your life. For maximum benefit, please keep your crystal grid intact for a minimum of 40 days.

## 8. *Use the power of a crystal to heal or open a chakra*

If you know that one or more of your chakras needs healing or there is a blockage of energy there, you can use crystals for this purpose too. You must choose a crystal corresponding to the color associated with the particular chakra. Here is a quick guide for each of the seven chakras:

The root chakra (the first chakra) is associated with the color red, and the crystals that work best are red garnet, smoky quartz, red jasper, hematite, etc.

The sacral chakra (the second chakra) is connected with the color orange, and crystal for this include carnelian, amber, orange calcite, goldstone, tiger's eye, etc.

The solar plexus chakra (the third chakra) is linked to the color yellow. The crystals for healing or unblocking the energy in the third chakra include yellow jade, pyrite, rutilated quartz, etc.

The heart chakra (the fourth chakra) is connected to two colors, pink and green. The heart chakra crystals include amazonite, emerald, green calcite, aventurine, rose quartz, etc.

The throat chakra (the fifth chakra) is linked to the color blue. The crystals for the throat chakra include kyanite, Angelite, apatite, sodalite, aquamarine, etc.

The third eye chakra (the sixth one) is associated with the purple color. Crystals that help in the healing of the sixth chakra include fluorite, amethyst, charoite, iolite, and more.

The last of the seven chakras is the crown chakra which is connected with the color violet and white. Crystals that work well this chakra are clear quartz, blue lace agate, ametrine, lepidolite, and more.

## 9. *Bury crystals under the earth to create a protective and/or empowering boundary*

You can bury quartz crystals at the four corners of a plot of land or any other space for protection as well as empowerment. For the protection of plots of land, it is best to choose large-sized crystals. The bigger the size of the crystals, the better protection your space gets.

It is important to clear, cleanse, and recharge the crystals before burying them. Also, transfer the power of your intention to the crystals. When you bury them, remember to keep the pointed side facing upwards for effective dissipation of negative energies and also to direct the attention of the universal energy for protection.

## 10. *Place crystals all over your body*

Placing crystals directly on your body has a completely different effect from that of holding them in your hands. For example, if you are looking to unblock the energies in a particular chakra, then take the chakra corresponding to that chakra, and place it directly on the body part connected to that chakra. This approach stirs up the energy vibrations in and around the chakra region and works with your emotions for healing and creating positivity.

For example, place an aventurine on your heart chakra to give and receive love. Place a quartz crystal on your crown chakra to receive guidance and enlightenment from the divine. If you meditate by placing an amethyst stone on your third eye chakra, your ability to enter a deeper level of consciousness increases.

Work with all the different ways mentioned in this chapter. Each situation calls for a different healing method. Additionally, you must include your intuition to check out what works best for you and your needs. Try all of them, and you will realize that some of the methods work brilliantly while some others give you average results. Experiment a lot, and don't forget to learn from each experiment.

# Conclusion

The power of crystals lies in their vibrational energies in their molecular system that has been set up within their system over millions of year. The color, the shape, and the property of each crystal and gemstone have been formed over millennia. They hold the natural energies of the Earth and the universe. The deeper crystals were buried in the depths of the Earth (thanks to natural pressure and heat applied on them), and more energy was accumulated in their molecular system.

The structure of the crystal system is such that the vibrational energy trapped within it can be aligned to optimize healing and well-being for the holder of the crystal. Crystals and gemstones work with various frequencies of vibrational energies and can use the resulting energy resonance to help you achieve your dreams and desires.

Depending on your thoughts, needs and willpower, the frequency of the vibrational energy of the crystal combines and interacts with the energy of your personal aura to help you realize your goals and intentions.

Every crystal's power is unique. The uniqueness is not restricted to one type of crystal, but every stone is different from another one. There will be similarities in the way they function. For example, two pieces of clear quartz can help bring clarity for you. However, each piece will work in its own unique way to perform this function.

The uniqueness of each crystal is so well defined that if you lose or damage a gemstone, then finding another one that gives out the exact same outcome as the lost one is impossible. You will simply have to accept something that works similarly.

A final point to remember is that crystals and gemstones cannot work their magic on their own. They need the energy of your powerful intention to help you achieve your dreams. Without your inner power, personal aura, and mental strength, crystals and gemstones will remain decorative items. So, delve deep, find your power, and multiply and magnify it with the help of crystals and gemstones.

# Resources

http://www.crystalage.com/crystal_information/crystal_history/
https://www.mindbodygreen.com/0-16394/how-to-choose-a-healing-crystal-thats-right-for-you.html
https://www.mindbodygreen.com/0-91/The-7-Chakras-for-Beginners.html
https://www.mindbodygreen.com/articles/how-to-recognize-when-the-universe-is-giving-you-a-sign
http://www.chakras.info/chakra-colors/
https://www.ethanlazzerini.com/crystals-beginners/
https://www.mindbodygreen.com/0-14044/10-crystals-that-will-make-you-healthier-happier.html
https://www.energymuse.com
https://www.gaia.com/article/crystal-care-clearing-cleansing-charging-your-crystals
http://www.thatcrystalsite.com/take-care-crystals-stones/
https://meanings.crystalsandjewelry.com/how-to-make-gem-elixirs-or-crystal-essences/
https://tesswhitehurst.com/the-10-best-ways-to-use-crystals-in-your-magical-and-spiritual-work/
https://www.energymuse.com/blog/using-healing-crystals/

Milton Keynes UK
Ingram Content Group UK Ltd.
UKHW041330190824
1311UKWH00054B/1085